The Future of Violence

BY THE SAME AUTHOR

America the Changing Nation
Frying Tonight

The Future of
Violence

BY

GERALD PRIESTLAND

'Forgive the man his violence . . .
For violence has a human face.'
>J. Bronowski: *The Face of Violence*

'If you wish for peace, understand war.'
>Liddell Hart: *Deterrent and Defence*

'It's us or them, isn't it?'
>An Ulster housewife

HAMISH HAMILTON
LONDON

First published in Great Britain 1974
by Hamish Hamilton Ltd
90 Great Russell Street London WC1

Copyright © 1974 by Gerald Priestland

SBN 241 02454 4

Printed in Great Britain by
Western Printing Services Ltd, Bristol

For my sons Andreas and Oliver:
that violence may spare them

Contents

Foreword

None of us lives and thinks in a vacuum, least of all a journalist like myself. A great deal of talking, reading and listening has gone into this book, and while I am grateful to many for helping me, I should be hard put to it to trace the origin of every idea here. However, I have appended a numbered reading list of some seventy titles which have been of special value to me, and where appropriate I have made attribution to them thus [17].

As on previous occasions in print, I must thank the British Broadcasting Corporation for supporting me with daily bread, while emphasising that the views expressed in this book are entirely my own, and that some of them are not of the kind I would think it proper to express elsewhere in my role as a staff broadcaster for the BBC.

And like any married author, I should express my thanks to my wife for tolerating a rival in the house all these months. It's over now, dear. She's left me for Hamish Hamilton.

Introduction

Whether or not this really *is* an age of violence it is certainly an age of crying conscience. There are too many things to weep over: Nature ravaged and poisoned, animals abused, men unmanned, women belittled, children stunted, noble cities brutalised. And though I grieve for all of these, it seemed to me futile to rage about them indiscriminately. So I determined some years ago to select as my personal adversary the mixed and manly evil of Violence. Professionally, from Belfast to Saigon, we were already well acquainted.

A reporter fails in his duty if his dispatches are overwhelmed by the tragedy—or comedy—of events. One's passions have to stay in the background. But time after time, moving on from one assignment to the next, I have felt scarred by what I have seen. It is right that a reporter should not pass judgment or advocate policy. But much of his work carries an implicit warning, a warning which too few people care to heed. After more than twenty years as a foreign correspondent, I feel about as influential as Cassandra at the siege of Troy. Surely not all our cries of 'Wolf!' have been false alarms? Or is the news really no more than entertainment? What has been the use of it all? Perhaps, in the end, to supply the experience and conviction for this book.

Behind it lie certain firm beliefs: that compassion is the highest virtue, and the infliction of unnecessary suffering the gravest wrong; that the one real heresy in human thought is to suppose that any significant issue can be simple, or any complex event have a single cause. I believe that human motives are almost always mixed; that a certain amount of conflict and tension is necessary to life; that we should all have smaller as

well as larger loyalties; but that (to quote that majestic Eliza-
bethan, Richard Hooker): 'Unless the last good of all, which is
desired altogether for itself, be also infinite, we do evil in making it our end. . . . Because in desiring any thing as our final
perfection which is not so, we do amiss.'[25]

If all this identifies me as unfashionably liberal and christian,
I shall wear the label without complaint; although I know
from experience that the middle of the road is the most dangerous place to walk.

I had written thus far when, in the Autumn of 1973, two things
happened to drive me on with a much deeper sense of personal
involvement. One was the Fourth Arab-Israel War, which
broke out not long after my younger son had returned from
visiting a kibbutz on the Golan Heights. The other event, which
gave me an even more compelling insight into the nature of the
violence in all of us, was my own depression, contemplation of
destroying myself, and eventual rescue from mental crisis. I
know that the crisis had been developing for many years: that
I had been punishing myself for the unforgivable sin of the
violence I felt towards others, and for the cruelty I believed I
had secretly inflicted upon them. A very personal matter, and
it may be that some will think it embarrassingly out of place, or
that it disqualifies me from attempting an objective analysis of
my subject. I think not. I know now that we must learn to live
with violence, or it will destroy us from within.

G.P.

CHAPTER ONE

An Age of Violence

I T IS popular wisdom that violence is the scourge of our time—spreading like the Black Death. Whether it takes the form of international warfare, civil commotion or individual mayhem, its reputation becomes more frightful every day. Vietnam, it is said, sardonically, has given War a bad name. Now the Middle East has given it a terrible repetitiveness. Elsewhere, civil war and crime seem to have become cross-bred, with bombings, kidnappings, extortion and hijacking spreading in all directions and for a wide variety of motives; while political robberies become hard to distinguish from straightforward bank raids. Looking through the headlines in a bad season, one might conclude that the world had been taken over by maniacs.

In Belfast, an IRA bomber dumps a shopping bag full of explosives in a restaurant and tiptoes away, leaving a random public to death and mutilation. It is almost a carbon copy of an earlier outrage against a floating restaurant in Saigon. At Lydda Airport in Israel, Japanese machine-gunners, hired by Palestine Arabs, mow down a flock of Puerto Rican Catholic pilgrims. In New York, three boys aged less than thirteen rape a seven-year-old girl on a slum rooftop and sling her body into the street below. In a London park, a group of teenage boys kick an old meths drinker to death, and laugh.

So violence is in fashion, or everyone believes that it is. Yet very few of us have any direct experience of violence to match our hatred of it. We are both afraid of it and largely inexperienced in it, gentle in our dealings with others, yet fearful how others may deal with us. Our convictions about violence are usually uncomplicated by much first-hand knowledge of it. Compared with our ancestors of A.D. 1250 or 1350 or 1450, we are soft and innocent.

For *where* is it violent today? Certainly not in middle-class North London, where I am sitting at this moment. The Metropolitan Police figures for violent robbery in the streets have recorded a 129 per cent increase in the past five years, yet London remains one of the quietest, safest cities in the western world. Robbery and allied offences still account for less than two per cent of all known crimes. In a population of seven and a half million, fifty violent robberies a week leaves the average citizen with an enormous margin of security. Still more does a rate of two murders-manslaughters-infanticides per week, a large proportion of which seem unavoidable in the sense of being committed by the insane or immediate suicides. With figures so small in proportion to the total population, a haphazard increase can cause sensationally misleading headlines. CITY MURDERS DOUBLE LAST MONTH — yes, from three, maybe, to six.

Timid Londoners may thank their family trees they were not born in Detroit. While London suffered 113 killings in 1972, Detroit had 601 in a population one-fifth the size of London's: a rate of one in every 2,500 citizens, against one for every 65,000 Londoners. The main reasons for Detroit's running bloodbath seem to be the turbulent immigration of poor blacks and whites from the South, and the casual availability of guns. But whatever they are, the results put British casualties in a certain perspective. So do the figures for accidental deaths in Britain: some 7,000 a year from road incidents, 900 from poisoning, 700 from burning, 500 from drowning. There appears to be a great deal less uproar about these forms of unnatural death, even though one might have thought them rather more avoidable than murder.

Even if it is true that the average American runs a greater risk of dying violently than the average Briton, those risks are unevenly distributed. The statistical John Doe might get killed once every four hundred years; but he could easily prolong his life by avoiding those most likely to do him in—his friends and relatives. British kith and kin are equally lethal.

Analysis carried out by the World Health Organisation in 1973 gave the United States a score of 6·4 fatal assaults per 100,000 people: high compared with the Irish Republic's score of 0·4, Denmark's 0·6, Italy's 0·9 and even Japan at 1·4 and

Australia at 1·5—but still outstripped by Venezuela with 8·4. The English-speaking countries as a whole are not in the top league of overall social violence, however, and probably never have been. American researchers[23] have even managed to devise scales of violence: top of the list for 1961–65 came the Congo (Zaire), followed by Indonesia, South Vietnam and Rwanda. Italy came 27th, France 29th, the United States 41st and Britain 74th. Three years later (after the ghetto rioting) the United States was rated 24th, and I dread to think where the United Kingdom of Great Britain *and Northern Ireland* would stand in the 1970–73 returns. And yet I still doubt whether the United States or Ulster could compete with the steady violence of South-east Asia, Central Africa or Latin America.

Restrict our view to Great Britain alone, and we should still be grateful we did not live earlier. It is many years since the British have seen a real riot (Notting Hill in 1958 scarcely deserved the name), and no one still living can recall troopers charging with drawn sabres or riflemen opening fire in English streets upon the mob. Yet many in authority seem to be haunted by the fear that, given an inch, chaos would march on Westminster once more.

Even our experience of war is fading. I myself was just too young to fight the Germans or the Japanese. Some of my classmates went on to skirmish with the Irgun, the Kikuyu, the Malay Chinese, Greek Cypriots, Indonesians and other colonial guerrillas. Frenchmen of my age have fought bloodily in Algeria and Indo-China, and Americans far younger will never forget Vietnam. But these were no longer total wars; their impact at home was political rather than military; they made no impact on the home fronts of Britain, France or the United States to compare with that of World War II. Today a Russian, German, Chinese or Japanese under the age of thirty-five will have had no serious practice in warfare at all—perhaps to the alarm of the professional military staffs concerned. From their point of view, there is a danger that young men will cease to take fighting for granted as a natural event in everyone's lifetime.

So what are we complaining about? What are we afraid of? Is this really an age of violence at all, or is it rather an age of unprecedented publicity, alarm and even unmanliness? Is it possible that so much talk about violence is really a symptom of its decline? Or, from a rather different point of view, is violence so terrible anyway? Has the corruption that some commentators see in our sexual behaviour infected our guts and our backbones too? Is our distaste for violence just a disguise for softness and cowardice? It is surely no coincidence that the People's Democracies, which loudly denounce militarism and war-mongering in the dithering Atlantic Community, do not allow such eccentricities as pacifism or conscientious objection in their own ranks. Peace to them means peace on their terms—or else. . . .

The problem of violence is an immensely old and complicated one. Its tide has ebbed and flowed through history, flooding now this country and now that. Throughout our study of it, it is essential that we keep our perspectives clear and our definitions sharp. Violence is the very opposite of reason: it is the compelling action resorted to when reason, through language, will not serve. So that in reasoning about it we must be specially careful of the irrational, violence's Fifth Column. Nowadays it can wear various masks: the mask of impatience to 'get things done', the mask of passionate devotion to a cause, even the mask of commonsense, distracting us from its true nature by saying, for example, that to insist upon evidence that the death penalty discourages murder is to perpetuate 'a dangerous superstition', the superstition of requiring proof.

I repeat: violence is an extremely complex thing. While we profess to dread it and denounce it, each one of us also entertains and enjoys it in some form. It is a magnet for hypocrisy. We are appalled at the thought of the youths who beat up old-age pensioners, and I have heard kindly old ladies vow they would take the greatest of pleasure in flogging the muggers till the blood flowed and they screamed for mercy. Human beings like you and me staffed the concentration camps of Nazi Germany, where more than seven million other humans died in degradation; and just forty years earlier, 26,000 Boer women and children perished in the British concentration camps in South Africa. It is a figure commonly cited,[39] that in the years 1820–1945, Man killed fifty-nine million of his fellow men.

I am not saying we are all guilty, but fewer of us are innocent than we like to think. Only a handful of sincere pacifists do not share the exhilaration that most of us find in 'a good war' for 'a just cause'. 'Now God be thanked who has matched us with His Hour,' crowed Rupert Brooke at the coming of the First World War, which in many ways was to be the most futile of all wars. The Italian Futurists hurled themselves with joy into the same ordeal, serving with distinction in what they called 'This wonderful, marvellous, terrible thing'. Their eventual patron, Mussolini, declared that 'only War brings human energies to their highest tension, ennobling those who dare to undertake it'. Nietzsche had sung of 'the good war which sanctifies any cause', and his moral descendant, Adolf Hitler, growled that 'Force is the first law . . . Struggle is the father of all things, virtue lies in blood'.

Our Victorian ancestors were capable of being loftily intellectual too in their justification of violence. That extraordinary prophet Winwood Reade[45] wrote scathingly of the 'sickly school of politicians' who maintained that 'all countries belong to their inhabitants, and that to take them is a crime'. On the contrary, said Reade, the conquest of Asia by the European Powers was a form of emancipation for them, the first step towards Asian nationalism. 'Thus war will, for long years yet to come, be required to prepare the way for freedom and progress in the East; and in Europe itself it is not probable that war will ever absolutely cease until science discovers some destroying force so simple in its administration, so horrible in its effects, that all art, all gallantry, will be at an end, and battles will be massacres which the feelings of mankind will be unable to endure.'

I quote from Reade's *Martyrdom of Man* not just to reveal his prescience (which is rather beyond my point) but to illustrate some of the cogent non-moral arguments that can be advanced in favour of War. How could Asia escape from tyranny and corruption, asked Reade, unless Europe set her free from them and laid the foundations of the nation state? Reade was a kind of Nietzschean social Darwinist, too. He thought a belief in God engendered 'a slavish and Oriental condition of the mind', and that Man would never reach his full powers until he had ceased to believe in a personal deity and in the immortality of the soul. 'The Unknown God' had decreed that Man should climb upwards on the miseries and agonies of the past; was it unfair that we, too, should suffer for the benefit of generations to come?

So it is possible to see War and other forms of violence as inevitable forces in the process of Natural Selection; as tools of historical surgery; as national stimulants; and they certainly have been all of these things, whether for the best or not. One of the frustrations facing modern Britain is that for more than a quarter of a century now there has been no overriding patriotic cause, no convincing external threat, to unite the nation, simplify our confused purposes and let off suppressed steam. Unlike the totalitarian countries, which always keep a bogey on the mantelpiece, we no longer know who our enemy is. In the past this has always been considered essential for defining our identity and drawing us outwards from parochial and family loyalties. At all levels violence can be an existential gesture, asserting and defining who and what sort of person one is—sometimes in defiance of reason.

Violence, it seems to me, can be offered on two overlapping levels: it can be action, intended to achieve a specific physical result like the occupation of territory or the killing of people; and it is a means of expression resorted to (as I have said) when language will not serve. The two levels may be combined; but there are occasions when violence is done not because anyone really wants to destroy a particular object or person, or considers that useful in itself, but because he does not believe his point of view can be communicated to his opponent in any other way.

I have said we must get our definitions clear: and one of the first things to define is whether, at any given time, we are talking about violence among nations (that is, War), violence among groups within nations (for example, racial or religious rioting), or violence among individuals (at its worst, murder). All three are violent, but we treat each category differently and even make distinctions within them—distinctions between liberation movements and terrorism, defensive war and aggression, murder and manslaughter. The varieties of violence are endless, the possible answers to them infinite, and it is naive to treat them as if they were all alike. It is part of my purpose to try to bring some order to the depressing scene by tracing the relationships and distinctions between these three categories of violence—among nations, among groups and among individuals.

And where do we draw the line between 'violence' and 'force'? The criminal, the terrorist, the psychopath use violence, we tend to say, while the Police, the Army or the citizen acting in his own defence employ legitimate force (provided we can identify them with our own interests). The standard retort of the modern revolutionary anarchist, when denounced for resorting to violence, is that the violence of Authority differs from his own merely in wearing a uniform and hypocritically calling itself force.

The game of definitions is one in which the last hand is never played; but the anarchist position has been deliberately exposed by their own prophet, Georges Sorel[48], who frankly granted the distinction between force (used by the middle classes to enforce obedience to authority) and violence (used by the proletariat to smash it). And as Sorel observed as early as 1906, orthodox Marxists were all too ready to acquire and exercise force in just the same way as the old bourgeoisie. He deplored the fact that Marx himself failed to appreciate the difference between middle-class force and proletarian violence. But then this is always the trouble with class-oriented definitions: it is invariably the middle classes who make them up.

Sorel, like most extreme revolutionaries, was a rigid puritan. Socrates, he considered, richly deserved to die for corrupting the youth of Athens with his permissiveness. But Sorel despised the bourgeois passion for peace at any price, and for everything that discouraged violence, attributing it to the disappearance of corporal punishment from French schools and to the general liberalising of the ways in which French children were brought up. But why, he asked, *should* peace be considered the greatest of civilised blessings? Why *should* any act of violence be regarded as a return to barbarism? Proletarian violence was totally different from the parodies of middle-class revolution. It was an act of war aimed at total destruction, not at the replacement of one minority tyranny by another.

The genuine, spontaneous uprising of the masses is a total myth; but the myth—the symbolic event that may or may not have taken place—was of supreme importance to Sorel and to those who have followed in his footsteps. Sharpville, the Dublin Post Office, the Boston Tea Party, the Munich Olympics Massacre—revolutionaries have always recognised the baptismal significance of violence: it is a crucial step towards the destruction of reasoned argument and compromise. Not just revolutionaries, but groups as diverse as young African warriors and teenage motor-cycle gangs have prescribed acts of violence as the key assertion of identity. Unlike an oath, a signature, or a sprinkling of water, an act of violence cannot easily be undone or forgotten.

For when it comes to the action, it is characteristic of violence that it seems to take control of us, not we of it. It transfigures the perpetrator, and there are physiological reasons why this is so. Many of our physical activities are preceded and conditioned by chemical changes in the bloodstream. Anger, fear and frustration, which commonly instigate violence, seem to increase the pressure and pulse of the blood, raise the glucose content, speed up the breathing and shut down the digestion. The nerves appear to be partially anaesthetised in some way, so that we have a courage and tolerance of pain which in normal times we would not think ourselves capable of. Most of these phenomena seem to be controlled from an area at the base of the brain which, recognising a challenge to the individual, responds by signalling for the release of noradrenalin and other hormones from the adrenal glands. The effect of these is rather like an injection of drugs: once in the bloodstream they are hard to resist and cannot be neutralised at will. A man who has been in a fight is not his normal self, and will not return to that state until the hormones wear off. A man who has been stimulated to *expect* a fight will often go looking for one, or for some energetic substitute, because his system is crying out for violent release.

The middle-class British family—perhaps less so the American—has been brought up to regard such feelings as sub-human, animal, something we should be ashamed of and learn to suppress. We do not really understand what is going on when these feelings are triggered; consequently we fear them. And this fear of being possessed by some primitive demon, in ourselves as much as in others, makes it all the harder for us to deal constructively with the problem of violence. This is part of the conservative predicament in arguing that the whole structure of society is threatened by violence and must be preserved by discipline: a discipline backed by force, or, failing that, by violence.

Instinctively we look for scapegoats. A car-bomb explodes in Coleraine, Northern Ireland, butchering six people in the street. A mob of coloured teenagers attacks a police car in South London. In Worcester, a man seizes three tiny children from their beds, violates them, gives each one a brutally different death and impales their bodies on a garden fence. Who, what, is to blame for all this? Horrified by the stirrings of dark forces within us as we visualise these outrages and either participate vicariously in them or avenge them in our imaginations with further atrocities, furious at the allegation 'we are all guilty', we rush to establish our moral alibis. We must blame such violence on people or forces that are totally *other* than us. The merciless punishments we demand for the culprits could only be inflicted upon people who were totally alien to us, almost another breed.

And yet from time to time we are forced to recognise that this is not so, that acts of criminal violence are committed by creatures of our own race. The explanations of social, emotional or economic deprivation point back towards the guilt of all society, and are thought to be unfair to the law-abiding, and so a less personal scapegoat is sought. The favourite at the moment is the Mass Media: the Press, Radio, Cinema and Television. The implication is that if only these could be restrained, violence would diminish and sound morals, strong authority, be restored. Why the Media are not also blamed for road casualties, divorce, environmental pollution and inflation escapes me.

Most ostentatiously violent (partly because it is a showy and self-advertising medium) is the cinema. In the late 1960s and early '70s, films like *Bullitt*, *The Wild Bunch*, *Soldier Blue*, *The Devils*, *A Clockwork Orange*, *Straw Dogs* and *Last Tango in Paris* provoked a long outcry for, allegedly, stimulating violence by their own show of callous brutality. Never mind that most of the outcriers never saw the films in question: what is more puzzling is that of all the media, the cinema is the one whose audiences and hold upon the public have been declining the most steeply. It is also the most public of them, and I suspect that while this makes it more of an emotional escape or outlet for the average viewer—and hardly an incitement at all—it also makes the offended spectator feel the greater need to repudiate what gives him offence.

One is entitled to ask: if the Mass Media *are* responsible for the increase in violence today, what can have caused the up-surges of (say) the American race riots of 1917–21, in which more than a hundred Negroes were killed; or the deaths at Peterloo, in Manchester, in 1819; or, come to that, the peasant revolts and religious slaughters of the Middle Ages? Why should our generation be any less violent simply because another splinter of Man's two-million year history has worn away? There was no Television in the days of Jack the Ripper, and fundamentally the London murder rate has not altered much since then—capital punishment or no capital punishment.

I am not arguing that because there has always been violence, there always should be violence and that it can never be reduced. Nor do I believe that the Mass Media are completely uninvolved in the causes of violence. But I do not believe, either, that they can invent what is not already about us. The Media are mirrors: sometimes rear-view mirrors, sometimes distorting mirrors and sometimes burning-glasses—but there must be something there for them to reflect. I believe most strongly of all that it is not what the Media say and show that alters our lives, but what actually happens in the real world. The Media report change, however; that is what news is. Those who dislike change often confuse reporting it with causing it.

At this point I think it important to stress the physical nature of violence. To some this will seem an evasion, an endorsement of economic or bureaucratic tyranny, like the refusal of the Soviet Government to allow dissident intellectuals to publish their manuscripts or emigrate to Israel. Martin Luther King used to insist that it was violence to deprive a Negro child of decent food and schooling. With great respect, I must disagree. Naturally I cannot endorse those or any other form of blatant injustice. Violence does overlap with coercion, persecution and cruelty; but it is not identical with them. All cruelty, all un-loving administration of suffering, is wrong (and why it is wrong leads us into the entire moral philosophy of liberal christianity). But the essence of violence is that *physical* power is deliberately employed, with the ultimate sanction of *physical* pain, and little choice but surrender or *physical* resistance (though we shall examine the non-violent or pacifist alternatives in a later chapter).

Through violence, a conflict is reduced to purely physical terms. The practitioner of violence is saying to his opponent: 'No matter what your metaphysical or moral rights and merits, my physical superiority obliges you to yield to me. We are removing this conflict to a different plane. You must abandon your will to mine.'

He who resorts to violence is thus renouncing the use of reason, persuasion or prayer and putting his antagonist in a lower category than himself. He may feel he has been driven to it, that the other man began it all, and that he himself is acting reluctantly and in self-defence. But invariably the other side is described as 'unreasonable'. Words no longer meet the case. The other man has ignored or rejected the arguments and misread the signals. No other course is left but violence—which would here almost certainly be termed force.

If we really felt that our enemy, our victim, was like our-selves—having the same feelings, hopes, rights and dependents—empathised with him, loving our neighbour as ourselves and putting ourselves in his place, we could not do to him what we would not choose to have done to us. Some of us retain that ability in spite of everything, a point worth recalling when faced with the claim that Man is inherently vicious. But almost every outbreak of hostilities between nations, every campaign of repression against a minority or act of individual violence, is accompanied by a conviction that the opposing party is a lower form of life—'dirty Jews', 'pigsty Pakkies', 'slant-eyed Gooks'.

I have gone on in this rather abstract way in order to make the point that there can be little direct, causal relationship between violence and the Mass Media. If the papers and broadcasting really were dismissing reasoned argument and representing certain sections of humanity as less than human, then they might well be accused of preparing the ground for violence. But in Britain and America at least the very opposite

is true. It is the Media above all which have tried to cultivate
sympathy for the Biafrans, the Bengalis, Uganda Asians, gip-
sies, Ulster Catholics and inner-city coloured people, and which
have tried to present rational analysis of social problems. It is
a very long time since the western world had anything like an
inflammatory press. As for broadcasting, it has been persistently mealy-mouthed.

And yet there come to hand, as I write, documents like the
Annual Report of the Chief Inspector of Constabulary for
England and Wales (excluding London), 1972. The Chief
Inspector, Mr J. M. Hill, records an increase in violence
against the person from 39,000 cases in 1971 to 44,000 cases in
1972, including a 21 per cent increase in robberies and assault
with intent to rob. It is worth noting that traffic accident casualties during the year 1972 totalled 360,000—including 7,700
deaths and 91,000 serious injuries. Publication of these figures
was followed by renewed argument about how to deter criminal
violence; but no headlines at all about the much heavier
casualties suffered on the roads. Perhaps this is because while
everyone wishes to dissociate himself from the mere criminal,
most of us nowadays are motorists. Perhaps it also tells us something about the degree of violence we consider normal in a
motoring society.

What Mr Hill finds most disturbing lies in the criminal
figures: 'a mindless aggression towards property or persons,
with no apparent motive other than possibly a general grudge
and antagonism against society as a whole.' Violence he sees
manifested in a variety of forms: battered wives and babies,
hooliganism, vandalism, mugging and the communal violence
of Saturday football crowds. Once it was believed that anti-
social behaviour was the result of poverty, and that it would
decline with rising standards of living and education. Unfortunately, reports Mr Hill, that expectation has not been
fulfilled. Perhaps, he suggests, the blame lies with television,
the cinema and the other Mass Media, through which we are
able to indulge our basic instincts, with the danger that the
more impressionable will seek to imitate in real life what they
find so absorbing on the screen.

There is no mention here, or in most social critics, of the
effect of ordinary human contact, of conversation, gossip, local

example and tradition as a means (and possibly the most important means) of spreading behaviour patterns. Yet I believe this is how mugging, bovver-boots and 'Pakki-bashing' really catch on, long before the newspapers find out and television purloins the story from the Press. But perhaps the first comment to be made on the Chief Inspector's diagnosis is that poverty is relative. Those lowest down the ladder consider themselves poor, however many rungs up they are. The poor in America today have cars and television. The poor of Britain have electricity and running water. None of them is poor by the standards of the Calcutta beggar with one soiled loincloth and a straw mat on the pavement for the night. It is not poverty as such but the sense of injustice, boredom and meaninglessness that works up the 'general grudge and antagonism against society as a whole'.

Could it even be that society as a whole really *is* antagonistic towards those we so deplore—particularly towards the young men and boys between the ages of ten and twenty-six who account for so large a proportion of violent crime? I shall return shortly to my defence of the Media, because I think the pursuit of fashionable scapegoats not only cripples the largely innocent beasts themselves (which is a pity), and fills the pursuers with undeserved and fatuous satisfaction, but also distracts effort from the real battlefield, which *is* society as a whole, with all its interlinked and interdependent facets.

But if single causes of violence are to be picked out one at a time, why not our economic system, with its mysterious mechanisms for deciding prices and rewards, and its constantly rising expectations, fanned by provocative advertising? It should not be difficult to prove a statistical correlation between the volume of advertising and the rise of personal violence. So why not blame advertising?

Or why not *blame* education and affluence, instead of citing them as discredited cures—blame them for encouraging materialist passions and giving people ideas above their station? Or town planning, for turning our cities into dehumanised zoos? Or the churches, for abandoning the moral sanctions of hell-fire? Or science, for undermining the myths of religion? Or the law, for playing with words while the guilty go free? Or modern nutrition for pumping too many vitamins and too much protein into our children? Or medicine, for lowering the infant death-rate of the socially undesirable? Perhaps, before long, someone will be brave enough to put in print the unspoken conviction of many law-abiding middle-aged folk: that it is all the fault of this democratic, socialistic nonsense about one man, one vote and everyone being as good as everyone else. In the old days, people knew their place and there was natural discipline. What we need is discipline again. In the meantime, let's knock the Media into shape; then perhaps the news will improve.

I may seem to have pilloried these points of view, as each one deserves to be pilloried if presented as the one great truth. But in fact there is an element of truth somewhere in each one of them, and they are all interconnected. The Mass Media help to connect them.

Personally I have many criticisms to make of the old-style journalism which has lived off the British public for the past fifty years and more. Still dominated by a philistine provincial tradition, insultingly cretinous and uneconomic to boot, the popular press is now largely incapable of dealing with long-range trends or unsensational developments at home or abroad. Stuck in a style developed for semi-literates early in the century, our popular papers present life as a series of smart, zippy revue sketches, each with a punchy lead and a simplified plot. There is no place for depth of understanding, thoroughness or good writing. Brightness and speed are all. But with all these faults it is very hard to see how our sex-loving, royalty-hunting, trivia-peddling press can be held remotely responsible for the muggings in the park or the bombings in Ulster.

What about television, then, the newcomer in the rogues' gallery of the Media? Nobody watches more violence on tele-vision than the Americans; and no one has done more research on the effects of it—thousands of closely printed pages of a thoroughness and dullness that only Americans can achieve or tolerate.

The Report of the Surgeon General's Scientific Advisory Committee on Television and Social Behaviour (*Television and Growing Up*[50],) reckoned an average of eight violent acts on the screen per hour during the period 1967–69—cartoon films being the most violent category. There was no doubt that violence was enormously popular and commercially successful:

far more so than sex, as any exhibitor or distributor of films knows, though I doubt if it follows that violence is more indulged in by the public than sex. On the contrary, it is the forbidden, the impossible, the remote that people want to see.

After all its chomping and chewing of experimental data, the Surgeon General's Committee pronounced: 'We can tentatively conclude that there is a modest relationship between exposure to television violence and aggressive behaviour or tendencies,' *but* 'there is evidence that any sequence by which viewing television violence causes aggressive behaviour is most likely applicable only to some children who are predisposed in that direction'. In other words, violent children may be stirred up by violent television, but it is not necessarily television that has made them incline to violence.

For the space in between the two conclusions quoted above is crowded with reservations. The 'modest relationship' takes the form of statistical correlations, most of which are 'of low magnitude' and none of which can prove that either factor, the viewing or the violence, actually caused the other.

Even if the relationships were much stronger than they are, the truth might lie in any one of three conclusions: that viewing violence leads to aggressiveness, that aggressiveness leads to the viewing of violence, or that both the viewing and the violence, while going together, are the result of something else. That might be an acquired or inherited characteristic established in the child long before it saw its first flickering screen; or it might be the child's communication with its parents (or lack of it), or its parents' own attitude towards punishment, towards physical expression, towards the showing of affection or the cultivation of gentleness.

Much has been made of one survey cited by the Committee, a study made by M. Lefkowitz and his team of the effects of viewing violent television programmes upon 211 boys from a rural New York county. It was a unique effort to follow the question over a long time-span, covering the boys' development from the age of eight to the age of eighteen. Complete interdependence between violence-viewing early in life and violent performance later would have produced a 'correlation coefficient' or index of 1·0. Lefkowitz got one of ·31, which was not insignificant in view of the numbers involved.

However, the results become less obvious the more one looks into them. The ·31 connection was only between viewing violence (according to reports by mothers) at the age of eight and acting violent (according to estimates by contemporaries) at the age of eighteen. There was no positive relationship at all between how the eighteen-year-olds were behaving and what the eighteen-year-olds were at that time viewing. And, strangely, if viewing violent television at the age of eight *had* produced violence at eighteen, the relationship in a given child was *stronger* than it had been ten years earlier (when there was only a ·21 correlation).

The Committee had doubts about the Lefkowitz data, too: a good deal of them seem to have been measured on rather subjective scales, and the ·31 coefficient 'depends almost entirely on a small number of boys who scored extremely high on the measure of aggressive behaviour. Without question, these boys would justify individual case study,' observed the Committee, 'but there appears to be hardly any relationship elsewhere in the range'. There may have been a tendency to build a law on exceptional cases.

Perhaps the most valuable thing about the Lefkowitz study— far more valuable than the early cartoon-watching habits of rustic hooligans—is its ability to predict, from the eight-year-olds' reputations for aggressiveness, who is likely to be violent at eighteen. Many psychologists would argue that eight is almost too late—that the damage had been done much earlier. But it might be a better investment for society to conduct that kind of research than to fret over the influence of Tom and Jerry.

Lefkowitz does admit that he has not eliminated the possible influence of parental emphasis on gentleness or aggression. One other team of researchers, under J. McLeod, did enquire into this factor elsewhere. They found that while there was a rather similar ·26 correlation between viewing violent television and acting aggressively in families where little emphasis was laid upon gentle behaviour, in families which actively cultivated gentleness the coefficient was only ·07. Surprise! Surprise! Violence may actually have something to do with the way a child is brought up by its elders! A. S. Neill, the ancient and celebrated Head of Summerhill, 'the school with no rules', firmly believed that the first slap on a baby's bottom is its induction to a life of violence. There is, he declared, less violence in Hampstead than in the slums of Glasgow, for the simple reason that there is more parental brutality in the Gorbals. Ninety-six out of a hundred Scottish schoolteachers want the power to beat primary school children; yet, said Neill, when the beaten boys take to mugging, the teachers can't see the connection.

Very well, then: since I am clearly not going to concede that television makes muggers of our children in the long run, what about its more immediate effects upon their elders? Here again the Americans can provide the scholarship, in the Report of the National Commission on Civil Disorders, which was specifically asked what effect the Mass Media had had upon the terrible ghetto riots of 1967. After much enquiry the Commission, which would have been only to glad to find a scapegoat, concluded that while the Media had generally exaggerated the troubles, had sometimes been sensational and inaccurate about them, and had been persistently superficial about the origins and consequences of the riots, they had not been a cause of them. It would be irrelevant to British readers to cite yet another of these ponderous American reports, were it not for the fact that similar accusations of spreading the trouble have been made against the British Media in Northern Ireland and during picket-line skirmishes in England.

Can it never be true that, at the sight of a camera, agitators whip up scenes of feigned desperation or provoke the police into acts of well-deserved 'brutality'? Of course it is sometimes true, and television men have become increasingly wise to it, as they have to staged events of all kinds. On the other hand, if we really are committed to the tolerant, liberal, open society and to a separation of powers between government and media— a separation which is more important to our liberties and more threatened by authority than the British public realises—then we must run a number of risks: and the risk that bad examples will get as much or more publicity than good examples is one of them. Moreover, if this really is a violent age or an age concerned about violence, neither print nor broadcasting will increase their credibility by pretending otherwise. The alternative is not so much censorship as some more subtle form of sterilisation like Guidance: guidance of the Media by those in power, and subsequently guidance of the public by the Media. It was one of the late President Nasser's most charming touches to call his Propaganda Ministry 'the Ministry of National Guidance'. It guided the Egyptian public from one disaster to another.

I may now seem incongruously to be placing religion and freedom of the press side by side. But it seems to me that anyone who wishes to arrive at an honest personal position on the problem of violence must incidentally make up his mind on two other points: whether he really does believe in liberal democracy (or in some more authoritarian politics), and whether there is any meaning in calling himself even a nominal, ethical christian. Public discussion of many subjects might make more progress if those involved came clean on these points.

Both christianity and liberal democracy are more vulnerable to violence, offer more openings to it, than their forceful rivals. That is not to say they are ultimately weaker (though too often that is not allowed to go to the test) but that violence commonly and sometimes intentionally has the effect of making people abandon milder ways and resort to counter-violence and tyranny, which in turn only produce more violence.

That is why, as we embark upon the following chapters, we must clothe our passion for peace in a certain coolness, even detachment. It would be a pleasure to release a cataract of rhetoric against violence—violence that is hideous because it enables the strong to destroy the weak, violence that reduces the finest works of Man and his noblest brains to pulp and rubble, violence that degrades reason to a shriek, innocence and beauty to rape-meat. But when all that is done, what is accomplished but an emotional purge, a passing fanfare that changes nothing? To achieve any practical good we must unearth every root and facet of violence, learn how it works and so how to control it. As the great anatomist of war, Liddell Hart, never tired of writing: 'If you wish for Peace, understand War.' To this I would add, understand Terrorism, understand Crime—understand their mechanisms and their true extent, unpanicked by the headlines and caring about individual sufferers as individuals, and not as symbols of some vast uncontrollable terror. Of course every case of mugging is an outrage. But even the Inspector General of Constabulary grants that Britain is very far from being a country where the average citizen should not dare to venture out alone at night.

I have suggested that one way to achieve clarity of understanding is to recognise a three-tiered structure of violence. There can be little doubt today that war is an unmitigated disaster—little, though there may be doubts about that in some militant states, and I am prepared to raise a question or two myself. How many of us are certain that World War II was not, when all's told, worthwhile? Or the Indo-Pakistan War of 1971, so far as Bangla Desh is concerned? But applied to highly developed powers like Western and Eastern Europe and North America, the prevention of war today must be at the top of every national agenda.

Most settled societies are just as anxious to prevent terrorism and civil strife. Ten or twenty years ago 'it couldn't happen here'. But today it *is* happening, and we need to think very carefully how we should deal with it. For if, like bodily fever, civil violence is the symptom of a disease throughout the organism, it will be false medicine merely to repress the symptom. And the same may well be true of violence among individuals. Here we must also distinguish between the normal human responses to anger, fear or frustration and the more alarming states of mental illness. We must recognise, too, that there exists today a malevolent philosophy of Violence Justified, with heroes like Fanon proclaiming that 'Violence alone, violence by the people, violence taught and organised by their leaders, makes it possible for the masses to understand social truths . . . binding the community together and committing each individual in his own eyes and those of others'.

The educational side of violence usually eludes the masses. For them it becomes a malignant spiral of action and reaction whose only merit is a release from the tedium of sterile argument. Once violence has broken out, as one observer of the Ulster scene has bitterly remarked, one needs only listen to one's own side of the case.

The temptation to do anything rather than continue verbalising is a road that forks right to violence, left to the mystical drug-hazy drop-out. There are so many voices straining to be heard, so few listeners, so little response; so much verbal trickery, so little attention paid to the teaching and practice of intellectual honesty and rational analysis, that it is sometimes a release to shut one's eyes and ears and mouth and draw one's sword.

CHAPTER TWO

The Roots of Violence

THE UGLY question is: Is Man violent by nature—innately, inherently, incurably violent as a species, the only one (it is said) that attacks and destroys his own kind, ultimately to the point where he may commit race-suicide and disappear from the face of the Earth, not because something higher has replaced him, but because nothing so evil could survive?

It is an appalling possibility, that we are doomed to be our own destroyers. To some people it is blasphemy, that God could have been so cynical as to create a nonsense in His own image. To others it is a sign of scientific impartiality, to be able to contemplate the coming Age of the Dolphin. The question of whether Man *is* by nature violent is a crucial one, because it tends to separate people into two exclusive streams: one pursuing the hopeful possibilities of redemption and reform, the other coldly analysing the facts. But there is also a third way between the two: that of asking how, even if Man is violent, that quality can be mitigated and controlled.

Human enquiry has always tended to follow waves of fashion which exclude each other. For many centuries Man thought of himself as Spirit, either of God's creation or his own. Then he became Will, either Marxist or Freudian. Now he is the human zoologist's Animal, the Naked Ape, and at last all barriers are down that prevented us from viewing ourselves as objectively as any other creature. The social anthropologists, ethologists and primatologists have generated much heat over the problem of human violence. Some have approached it by going far back to the bone deposits of southern Africa; others by extending present-day ape behaviour into our own pre-historical backyards. In neither case does it seem to me that the conclusions drawn can be strictly applied to ourselves in our own times and conditions; but they can be illuminating. For example, I think it would be hypocritical to deny that a monkey-like dominance system or pecking order *does* exist in most human organisations (though we have tinkered with it, through devices like seniority and democracy)—or that we, too, have our gestures of submission, warning and challenge (though we have confused them and overtaxed our understanding of them).

That record of the Jewish folk-memory called Genesis, which has become also the foundation of conscience for christendom, has no doubt that we are essentially violent, and were so from the beginning. The first active sin committed after Man's Fall was the murder of Abel by Cain; and five generations later, Cain's descendant Lamech was thundering out his threat to take vengeance seventy-seven-fold against any who dared so much as touch him—the first paranoid schizophrenic on record. In general, it does not occur to the Old Testament, nor did it to its readers for hundreds of years, that violence was anything other than natural and usually just. Tom Paine, of *The Age of Reason*[44], was particularly revolted by Numbers Ch. 31 vv. 17–18 (where Moses speaks angrily of the captured Midianites: 'Now kill every male among the little ones, and kill every woman that hath known a man by lying with him; but all the women-children that have not known a man by lying with him, keep alive for yourselves.') which Paine saw, with eminent reason, as 'an order to butcher the boys, to massacre the mothers, and to debauch the daughters'.

But perhaps the ancient Israelites were not typical of us in our innocence. Some anthropologists have cited the behaviour of certain passive, unwarlike tribes as proof that Man is not inevitably self-destructive. The Auroguacos of Colombia, if two of them quarrelled, would each take up a wooden staff and belabour a nearby rock or tree. The one whose stick broke first was the winner, and the two men would then embrace and return home reconciled. The Semai of Malaya are said to be incapable of using violence towards their children, with the result that the children grow up with no concept of violence at all and have to let off steam by exchanging insults and spreading malicious rumours about each other. The Abron, of the Côte d'Ivoire, direct their aggressiveness against imaginary demons (which they are never quite able to eradicate), and the Mru of the Chittagong Hills are so timid that when faced with a quarrel they call in a medium and ask the spirits who would win if there *were* to be a fight—a verdict they immediately accept. The Eskimos of the Arctic, and the Lepchas of Sikkim, simply have no social organisation for war. And the Chatham Islanders had a law most worthy of imitation: that all fighting must end when the first drop of blood was shed.

Alas, almost all of the peoples mentioned are vanishing or have already vanished. Not one of them is among the Top Ten nations of the world. There are at least as many examples on the opposite side of the ledger, appearing to illustrate the essential violence of mankind. To the Yanomamo Indians of South America, warfare is an almost permanent way of life. Many of their children are slain at birth, and a third of their adults perish violently in battle—yet they survive. The paradise of the South Seas, held up by Rousseau and his followers as the pristine example of Man's natural goodness when uncontaminated by false laws, was, in some of the island groups, an unequalled hell.

The chieftains of the Hawaiian Islands enforced their authority by an elaborate structure of *Tabus*, the penalty for breaking any of which was death—without trial or appeal. Death for allowing one's shadow to fall upon the chief or any of his possessions, death for entering his house through the wrong doorway or with a wet loincloth or an unwashed face, death for raising one's knee from the ground while the chieftain ate, death for launching one's canoe at the same moment as his, or for straying across the unmarked boundaries of his residence. Small wonder that a British officer who visited the islands in 1793 was sickened by the display of skulls and the stench of rotting corpses in the royal enclosures.

Things were, if anything, rather worse in Fiji[15] and certainly remained so for a good deal longer than in Hawaii. Not for nothing was the Fijian group avoided as 'the Cannibal Islands'. In the 1830s, and on into the '40s, the chiefs of Mbau (the sacred stronghold) held huge banquets of freshly killed and imported corpses. After the capture of nearby Verata in 1839, 260 bodies were distributed among the victors, and thirty young children were hoisted alive to the mastheads of the war canoes, where they were dashed to death by the winds during the voyage home. Captured infants were often used as practice victims, upon whom the sons of conquering tribes rehearsed the arts of killing and butchery. None of this was too surprising in a society where live burial of the sick and the strangling of widows by their elder sons were common. Today, I hasten to add, there are no more agreeable people to be found than the Fijians. Like the Hawaiians before them, they sickened in the end of their own cruelty and gratefully received the missionaries whose good works in the Pacific it is now fashionable to overlook.

Yet these pictures—on the one hand of extreme gentleness, on the other of acute savagery—are not so contradictory as might appear. Running through most of them is a need to find some way, violent or non-violent, of resolving conflict and ordering society. There are reasons for believing that the excessive cruelty of the Hawaiians and Fijians was a comparatively late aberration—like the excesses of Nazism—and that what we can still see today in the remote interior of Papua is a good deal more typical of natural, primitive Man. Here there is a good deal of inter-village and inter-tribal warfare, with two or three thousand warriors taking the field on some occasions. But the 'war' is largely a matter of chanting and posturing, sometimes of furtive ambushing, and casualties seldom take more than the fingers of one hand to count. Where there is cannibalism, it is almost a religious ritual, rather than a nourishing feast: it is either a form of insult to the dead or a way of absorbing his strength magically.

At this point I do not want to enter into the origins and nature of violence between nations; but primitive groups, different though their circumstances may be from ours, do remind us of one important factor that was clearly understood even in Europe not so long ago: that violence is often the limited climax to a formal expression or statement, that the preparations and formalities are frequently more important than the blow itself, which should not always be taken at its face value. This may not be of any comfort to the victims; but at times (and I think here of the Assam War between India and China) the apparent aggressor is only trying to make some point to satisfy some conception of national honour which has not been cleared by

normal communication. What happens often in primitive warfare is that a traditional procedure for resolving conflict has
broken down, and a physical substitute is then resorted to,
involving threatening displays, dressing up, insults and curses,
perhaps ultimately leading to some loss of life. The party then
breaks up. There is seldom any question of occupying each
other's territory, and none whatever of suppressing each other's
gods or ideologies. Violence is simply an extreme form of curse.

But let us get back to the individual again: why should he
strike his brother or his friend, never mind the stranger from
abroad?

It seems to me that the truly unique thing about Man is his
consciousness of himself as an individual, his ability to form an
almost-objective image of himself, and to select from the
various ingredients he can recognise in himself a particular
identity which he will cultivate and defend. That is not to say
that we all have the same ingredients in the same proportions,
or that we all try equally hard or are equally successful in
realising our choice. Some choices are contradictory and lead
to crippling conflicts within us. Some choices are imposed upon
us. From the moment of birth we are aware of a distinction
between what we want, or want to be, and what others more
powerful want. In working out our identity we can either con-
form to what is required of us, battle against it, or work out
some compromise.

It is a commonplace of psychology that violence against
society begins with the frustration of the infant by its father
and even more (in my view) by its mother: for whom Authority
later becomes a symbol and substitute. At once further contradictions arise: the individual wants to be loved and admired
(because this is not only sensually pleasant, but reassures him
of his identity), but he wants this on his own terms. Those who
fail to accept his terms must be made to suffer too, then they
will realise how he feels and thus who and what sort of person
he is. Love and hatred feed into each other. I have spoken of
violence as the physical language or tool of aggression, but I
have also described it as the *unloving* application of force. If
violence is to be more than mere force, it must have the color-
ation of hatred or unlove.

Because Man is born into a family, he also encounters a

contradiction between himself as a separate individual and himself as a member of a group. He wants to *belong*, but again, not on terms which restrict his autonomy. He may seek to resolve this by joining very small, select groups which closely reflect his own view of himself. Or the conflict may be resolved for him by those who choose for themselves the role of leader and succeed in binding together the group—it may be a nation, village, church or school—by establishing common interests and purposes and very often a common enemy.

So far we have been moving towards an explanation of aggression which can be summed up in the one word: frustration. Freud accepted this view early in his career, before he invented the bizarre concept of the Death Wish and found himself obliged to explain aggression as the reverse side of that never-very-convincing coin. The theory that aggression is always the result of frustration became vastly popular in the United States from the 1940s onwards. But does it in fact correspond with experience? Isn't the whole complaint against the Permissive Society based upon the observation that removing restraints does *not* eliminate violence and make men virtuous? Haven't we all met people who, whatever the circumstances, go round looking for trouble and picking fights? Later still in his career, Freud himself kept coming back to the conclusion that a powerful desire for aggression was part of Man's original endowment, 'innate, independent, instinctual. . . .'

A number of academic conflicts developed during the forties and fifties. Some psychologists argued that aggression was made worse by retaliation; others that, on the contrary, retaliation was a deterrent. American research was said to indicate that all aggression was a reaction to the environment; German and Austrian scientists bred rats that were still aggressive after being raised in isolation in completely neutral environments. But clearly if Man was innately aggressive, it still had to be shown why he was in terms of evolutionary needs, and what it was that triggered off acts of aggression.

A plausible answer was found among the animals. For generations life-scientists had studied our fellow creatures in the convenient but artificial surroundings of the zoo (Man, as a species, they had scarcely studied at all). Slowly they began getting out of the zoos and laboratories and into the field. A forgotten Afrikaaner named Eugene Marais was one of the first, though his observations of baboons in the wild, made very early in this century, were not available in English until 1939, after his death. Equally obscure was Henry Eliot Howard, a Birmingham businessman and amateur birdwatcher, who realised as early as 1904 that the reason birds sang the dawn chorus was not to express their *joie de vivre*, but to lay aggressive claim to *territory*. This challenged the classic Darwinian theory, that the key to the evolutionary contest was the sexual struggle for the best mates; but gradually even old-school Darwinians like the venerable Sir Arthur Keith accepted that the drive to hold territory was not only a proven instinct among animals, but the probable explanation for nationalism and war among human beings.

Two names loom large here: Konrad Lorenz, whose essential book *On Aggression* was originally published in Vienna in 1963,[30] and Robert Ardrey, a playwright by profession, whose three successive works, *African Genesis*[2], *The Territorial Imperative*[3] and *The Social Contract*[4] (though a trifle apocalyptic at times) have enveloped and in the best sense popularised the anthropological approach to our problem.

Lorenz does not believe that aggressiveness is a mere reaction to frustration. You can eliminate every frustration, he says, and still have aggressive people on your hands: perhaps what is wrong with modern Man is that he is denied sufficient outlet for his aggressive drive. It is not true, observes Lorenz, that Man is somehow unique and perverse among creatures in attacking and even killing his own species: many vertebrates do, especially under conditions of overcrowded territory. And it is clearly to the evolutionary advantage of the species if, through mutual antagonism and repulsion, groups can be spaced out over the available feeding grounds and not over-crowded.

With most social animals it is not necessary to go further than a growl and a show of teeth to enforce the territorial conventions. Animals of the same kind are either physically equal or ordered by rank—which reduces the point of fighting; and the more deadly the species, the more precautions seem to have been built into its behaviour to prevent it destroying itself. Lions and tigers rarely fight among themselves.

Man, however, is about the most ill-equipped creature for fighting that anyone could devise: thin-skinned, soft parts exposed, blunt badly-placed teeth, no horns, no hooves, no claws. He also seems to have lost the rituals and inhibitions that restrain the more lethally-equipped species. Perhaps we evolved physically when there was very little likelihood of our being able to destroy ourselves: the talents we have now developed for doing so were the very talents that enabled us to break away from the limitations of bodily endowment and master our environment instead of submitting to it.

I am not equipped to go into the question of what made Man a tool-maker (or, with more sinister significance, a weapon-maker). Some mutation to a big brain, perhaps, and with it a taste for the mixed, protein-rich diet that provided the brain with its fuel. Some of our ancestors were evidently cannibals, extracting the food for thought from their own relatives' crania. But once Man had learned to use weapons and tools to assert his concept of himself over his fellows, the rest of the story follows. All members of the species are no longer equal; and even though they never were in practice, because of the dominance hierarchy or 'pecking order', even rank is no longer dependable. The old insignia can no longer be trusted: a new weapon or superior skill in using it can give a small individual or tribe an unexpected advantage over a great one. The story of David and Goliath is significant not only for the history of Israel, but for that of all mankind: a symbolic insult by technology against Nature. By inventing weapons Man undermined the symbolic substitutes for violence with which Nature had endowed him, and opened up an endless future of ingenuity, uncertainty and suspicion. Even flight and fear were no longer respected.

This should be indication enough of the dangers of relying too much on baboon and monkey parallels to explain our behaviour. We are not in fact their descendants, but eccentric relatives going back perhaps to a common ancestor. And, as Ardrey points out, we are not just territorial, we are predatory, too: we prey upon others and their territory, and although we are happiest at home we have a long history of making ourselves at home in other people's.

We must always have been group creatures, living at first

in small tribes, divided up into the usual classes of elders, young braves and mothers with children. Some of our friction today is the result of uncertainty over the changing boundaries of these classes: when do youngsters cease to be children and deserve to be treated as young braves, and when do young braves graduate to being elders? Any group requires a nice balance between two qualities which the nineteenth-century polyhistor Herbert Spencer described as 'Amity' (with one's own group) and 'Enmity' (towards outsiders). Ardrey even develops this into a neat equation:

$$A = E + h$$

That is, Amity is balanced by Enmity plus hazard. Increase the Enmity from outsiders, and the Amity, or solidarity, of the tribe increases to compensate. A tribe facing great environmental hazards, it is argued, will look for few enemies. On the other hand, one with little hardship to face and no enemies is liable to find its social warmth and cohesion growing weak.

Ardrey himself admits that his formula is intended for illumination rather than prediction, and in so far as it is helpful it seems to me to apply to the individual as well as the group. Each one of us must contain a balance of contentment and restlessness to survive: the Enmity side of the equation might best be expressed as Ambition or Challenge. Which prompts the optimistic conclusion that if only the impersonal 'h' factor were big enough—the challenge of overcoming some problem, climbing some mountain—there would be little need for marking out particular human enemies.

It has been argued (by Lorenz among others) that our morals are essentially derived from the evolutionary needs of the group, and so (if we accept it) from the instinct for Territory. Back in 1864, Alfred Russell Wallace, a collaborator of Darwin's who actually invented the term 'survival of the fittest', wrote that mental and moral qualities were just as important for survival as physical characteristics: 'Capacity for acting in concert, for protection of food and shelter, sympathy, which leads all in turn to assist each other; the sense of right, which checks the depredation upon our fellows . . . are all qualities that from earliest appearance must have been for the benefit of the community, and would therefore have become objects of natural selection.' So much the better for the optimists, for here is another reason for supposing that non-violent behaviour is as much a part of our nature and interests as destructive behaviour. Yet there is still room for that conflict between the individual's view of himself as autonomous, and his view of himself as belonging to a group. The Middle Ages were right to treat Pride as the deadliest of the sins, for it expresses the individual's refusal to subordinate his will to that of the group.

Lorenz is inclined to take the blame back to something perhaps even more fundamental, to the development of conceptual thought and verbal expression, which he thinks may have been that Forbidden Fruit which led to our exclusion from the paradise of blameless instinct. Certainly, without thought and expression it would have been hard for Man to develop his fatal self-consciousness, to pass on and develop his material and philosophical inventions from one generation to another, and so outstrip his old embedded rituals and inhibitions. Yet our old endowment remains, and our inability to change it accounts for the fact that we so irrationally refuse to learn from History or follow our patent interests. The eminent Dutch professor Nikko Tinbergen[19] reminds us that biologically we are still Cro-Magnons: but we have changed our environment out of all recognition. Our instincts have been unable to keep up with the changes we have made in our social surroundings: that is why Man is a misfit in his own society and responds so often with violence.

I believe he does so very largely because he sees a threat to his complete identity. This threat could be described as a kind of frustration. A society as complex technically and socially as ours is bound to keep frustrating, or threatening, its children with endless commands not to do this or that, not to walk in the road, fiddle with the gas cooker, swallow Mummy's pills, put your hands inside the TV set, your head out of the car window or into a plastic bag, with the result that our childhood (prolonged almost beyond reason by formal education) is a continuous accumulation of frustrating negatives. There has been no compensating increase in positive opportunities for children to assert themselves. Which is not to say there should be no parental guidance or opposition: on the contrary, if there is nothing to push against or get a grip on, there is no real proof that the individual exists outside a ghastly solipsism. Some cases of violence are attempts to jolt the parent, or Authority, or the rest of society, into any kind of response at all—even a slap on the wrist.

Ardrey weakens his emphasis on Territory as his thought progresses. Identity, Stimulation and Security, he says, are Man's basic needs; and territory, place, home are all aids to the supreme need for identity. 'I am the man who lives here, is known here, belongs here.' This is followed by the need for Stimulation, which I would call a means of checking and exercising Identity. Security comes third, often sacrificed to the other two needs. The opposites, from which Man seeks to escape, are Anonymity, Boredom, Anxiety—all of which threaten to destroy his personal identity.

The groups to which most of us belong, from the family up to the nation state, have sought with fair success to bring us Security, which is no longer the major concern of most people in the western world. But in their success our communities have deprived us of a great deal of Stimulation and Identity. There can be no denying that violence and war are the most stimulating of all activities. Yet under the praiseworthy banners of Peace and Law and Order, our society is trying hard to suppress those opportunities too.

We also seek, as individuals, to stamp out violence in the infant. Grabbing food, defending possessions is as natural to a small child as it is to an ape, and it is scarcely fair to call such behaviour 'violence' at all, for there is no real hatred or unlove involved. Nevertheless authority is asserted, not just to ensure fair shares of the food or the return of a toy to its rightful owner, but to discourage the very show of instinctive force. There follows punishment, kicking and screaming, loss of love, and anxiety all round. Much is written about the long-term effects upon children of the guilt they acquire from suppressed aggressiveness, and of how it has to be got rid of—transferred or transformed by the psychological processes known as displacement and projection. But the effect upon parents of actually disciplining their children can be equally hard to live with. Children, instead of hating their repressive but beloved parents, may grow up to hate the Germans or the Jews, attributing to them the children's own malevolence. Parents, instead of loving the children who bring out the worst in them, may turn dumbly to their pets and gardens and motorcars for solace.

In spite of such complications the world is not, on the whole, an open Bedlam. Most of us learn to cope with these conflicts, though society hardly helps by requiring of us more bottling up of feelings than it is prepared to let us release through approved outlets. I think we have seen enough by now to realise that we must make the distinctions not only between force and violence (violence being the unloving use of force, and the physical language of aggression) but between aggression itself and *ambition*. Ambition is the drive to establish identity: it will not necessarily resort to violence unless it acquires hatred; and hatred is the result of identifying some other person or force as a threat to one's own identity. There can be no question, surely, that a reasonable degree of ambition is a good thing. Indeed, it lies behind everything that the individual, the culture, the species has ever achieved—from the Suez Canal to Beethoven's Ninth Symphony. Without it we should be no more than another line of feeding and breeding animals. But the selfsame ambitious drive which made Handel complete 'Messiah', Columbus seek a New World and the Wright Brothers defeat gravity also inspired Hitler, Stalin and Mussolini, and perhaps, too, Jack the Ripper.

But surely there is a difference between genius and madness?

It is necessary nowadays to begin any discussion of the abnormal or insane by insisting that there really *is* such a thing as normality, and not merely conformity. A normal person is one who has arrived at maturity without disaster, with a realistic view of himself and his powers, able to take care of himself and yet to enjoy relations with others, to give love and receive it. A normal person has managed to reconcile the various contradictions within himself, to preserve both his autonomy and his place in society, and to find a satisfactory expression of his chosen identity in the life he leads. Within this framework, none of us qualifies as one hundred per cent normal, and perhaps the greatest works are accomplished by those who are a long way from it; but there is an important distinction between a man and his works. Beethoven, for example, was hardly normal, but this does not detract from what he left us.

There is the modern school of R. D. Laing which argues that Abnormality is really a kind of *super*-normality, the stormy progress of the soul to a higher reality, the breakdown that must go before the rebuilding and rebirth of the personality; rather as the advocates of psychedelic drugs used to urge the taking of LSD in order to 'blow the mind' and penetrate to the inner Truth. There is no arguing with mysticism. But most people who have had experience of the mentally ill and the drug-addicted find Laing's view hard to accept: principally because we cannot (perhaps dare not) will that such loneliness, lovelessness and inability to intermesh with the rest of the world should be left to march on to its own destruction.

There really are mental abnormalities and illnesses, just as there are (*pace* Mrs Eddy) physical ones, and it is perverse to pretend otherwise. How the upsets of the mind are classified, so early in the science, is partly a matter of fashion: there are the less severe *neuroses*, which do not entirely incapacitate and of which the sufferer is usually aware. More serious are the so-called *psychoses*, or severe disorders which urgently need attention, though the victims may not acknowledge them. Some may have physical causes: brain damage or tumours, glandular malfunctions, drugs, alcohol, even diseases like syphilis. The Californian allergist Benjamin Feingold believes that the chemical *salicylate* which appears in a large number of artificial colourings and flavours is responsible for much wilful hyperactivity in children: who knows what other additives may be doing? Evidence has been produced recently that links some violent psychoses with the virus *herpes simplex*. And some extraordinary work done at the University of Miami seems to confirm the theory that, every fourteen months or so, the combined tidal pull of Sun and Moon upon the Earth produces a definite increase in ruthless and bizarre crimes of violence. The effect seems to be upon their quality, more than their quantity.

Looked at another way, people may be described as suffering from relatively unobtrusive *character* disorders, or from deep *personality* disorders which make a considerable impact. There are schizoids, who distrust their fellow beings and withdraw, sometimes into delusions of power. There are hysterics, who love to dramatise their brittle lives. There are obsessives, who are often emotionally crippled and devote themselves furiously to the care of the unimportant. There are depressives, who have been unable to come to terms with the potential violence within, and try various forms of punishing themselves. And, familiar to us in crime, business and politics, are the paranoids (or paranoid schizophrenics) who express their distrust of others by turning the situation round and accusing the others of malicious conspiracy against them. Any of these types may end up committing violence. But in general their disorders represent attempts to find a formula for life which will *not* lead to destruction.

There remains the most dangerous of all, the psychopath or sociopath, the 'seriously irresponsible' as British law terms him, who expresses his aggression not in forms disguised so as to be socially acceptable, but directly and openly. He is the shark in the oceans of society, the destroyer, the killer, utterly without shame or inhibition.[24] In the early nineteenth century he was sometimes described as 'morally insane', because while he was not, by most definitions, medically insane, he showed no concern with morals and no understanding of their significance. They might apply to others, but not himself.

'Psychopath' is still a rather vague expression. A number of psychopaths show abnormal brain-wave readings and may even have damaged brains, but this is not invariable. Many have suffered abuse and rejection in early childhood; unloved, they are incapable of loving. They have no care for the feelings of others, and no anxiety about themselves. They yield recklessly to the impulse of the moment, regardless of consequences, and they emerge without pity or guilt. They are the very opposite of the neurotic, whose burden of guilt often paralyses him into complete inactivity. The psychopath, on the contrary, is a very busy man. He craves excitement, and often makes his first appearance in the Police files as a dangerous driver. He is unhampered by any feeling that he should be fair to others, take their point of view, respect tradition or avoid giving offence. Truth means little to him: he will batter, rape and kill and deny it all, for he is often incapable of telling fact from fantasy. He does not even feel depressed or persecuted when he is caught. He lies and betrays cheerfully. Yet, although he is incapable of truly reciprocal friendship, he can inspire intense devotion in others to the extent of hero-worship: for he is decisive, he acts, he gets results while others are dithering, and being without fear he makes a heroic leader be it in business, politics, war or crime.

How can such a monster ever survive? Because to many he does not appear a monster. Since he despises others, his pleasure is magnified by deceiving them: only *he* knows how powerful he really is and how pathetic they are. The psychopath is cunning, plausible, even charming. Time and again the closest acquaintances of convicted psychopaths cannot bring themselves to believe what has been proven. 'He was such a charming man,' they say—or 'He was so quiet, so fond of children.'

There has been someone to say that of almost every famous monster in history, from the fifteenth-century Marshal Gilles de Rais (who debauched and massacred perhaps 140 young children), to Nathan Leopold (of Leopold and Loeb; an intellectual genius who killed to prove himself a superman above the law), to John Reginald Christie (who quietly committed at least eight murders), John George Haigh (who drank his victims' blood), Ian Brady and Myra Hindley (the Moors Murderers), Lee Harvey Oswald (who shot Kennedy), and especially Charles Manson of California, whose infatuated 'Family' of runaway girls butchered perhaps eight victims at various times, including the beautiful (and pregnant) film actress, Sharon Tate.

None of these, it must be emphasised, was a 'typical' murderer; and yet we tend to think of such cases when murder is being discussed. We do so largely because they are exceptional —for literary and dramatic reasons rather than because they represent significant numbers of imitators. The typical murderer today kills, often quite openly, a close friend or relative, in a fit of temper. Usually he is overwhelmed by terror and remorse. Quite often he kills himself. He does not plan in advance and he does not repeat a pattern of killing. I am concerned here with the stars of our Chamber of Horrors partly because I want to put them in perspective as criminals, and partly because I want to point out the significance today of the *consciously* paranoid and psychopathic approach (if this isn't contradiction in terms).

First let me recall how some of our star monsters behaved: Charles Manson was the son of a sixteen-year-old street girl, who received his education in reform schools, prisons and drug communes. In the Haight-Ashbury quarter of San Francisco, in the mid-1960s, it was not difficult for him to become a leader among the drop-outs and drug addicts: most of them were desperate for some kind of older father-figure and saviour, and too demoralised, disoriented and befuddled to resist his mumbo-jumbo appeal. He had an ear open to the fashions of the day, and like many of that generation he and his followers were fed up with abstract verbalising and turned to the instant Zen of sex and drugs. These were the foundation of almost everything the Family did, and upon them Manson went on to erect a mythology of himself as a hip Messiah who would unleash a judgment of blood upon corrupt America and punish those who had underestimated and despised him all his life. What he would demonstrate to them was his *power*— such power that he did not need to do any killing himself, but could dispatch girl disciples to do it for him. Three of them, and one male disciple, bloodily executed Sharon Tate and her guests and then returned to base to make love with their leader. The following day, he had them kill again: a supermarket owner and his wife, selected at random.

At their trial, the Family tried to turn the case against Society. As Colin Wilson points out[58], Manson obscenely parodied the theory of Herbert Marcuse, that the free democratic society of America had become as dictatorial and repressive as Nazi Germany or Bolshevik Russia, and that revolution alone could burn out the rot. 'You made your children what they are,' Manson told his judges. 'The parents kicked them out and I did the best I could with them. . . .' One of the girls who had helped to kill Sharon Tate, asked if she thought the massacre of eight fellow beings 'unimportant', demanded in return whether the massacre of thousands of Vietnamese peasants with napalm was unimportant? It was dislocated, anarchic reasoning; it kicked aside the entire basis of law in a christian society, which is that the individual matters as much as the state, the mass or the class, if not more. But her retort brought cheers from young Americans from coast to coast.

Alas, it was only an extreme example of the perverted forms which argument is now assuming everywhere: driven not by the desire to uncover objective truths or practical possibilities but by the urge to score emotional points. To allow full licence, Reason is trussed away in a cupboard and a harlot installed in her place. The subject is changed, personality exploited, false analogies are drawn, prior conditions demanded, motives are impugned and shibboleths nailed to the flagpost as 'not negotiable'. Behind it all lies the exasperated feeling that there *is* no truth, no reason—only power. Yet it is the barrenness of this false argument, not of true reason, which destroys our confidence in it. It has become both a cause of revolt—and a favourite weapon of revolutionaries.

Ian Brady, the Moors Murderer, was the illegitimate son of a nineteen-year-old Glasgow waitress, a slum child who felt himself despised by better-class schoolmates. His first appearance in court was at the age of thirteen, and his life progressed drearily through probations and Borstal until he became a clerk in a Manchester chemicals firm at twenty-one. The North of England is no place for hippy communes or camping in the open like Manson: Brady got his inspiration not even from films or television, but from the worthy medium of print. His schoolteachers might have been proud how much he read, provided they had not seen the titles and authors: books about Nazism, torture, concentration camps, de Sade. The more he read, the more Brady felt he had found the truth at last: that life was corrupt and meaningless in the long run, and that only the ruthless could hope to gain any pleasure, by taking what they wanted without pity. As sexual partner and disciple, Brady acquired one of the office typists, Myra Hindley. First he dominated her, then he seduced her and educated her; finally they abducted, killed and buried at least five young people, making photographs and tape recordings of some of their perverted rituals.

To continue this parade of methodical butchery—through Christie and his gassings, Richard Speck who ravished and slew eight Chicago nurses in one night, Charles J. Whitman who shot forty-four people (thirteen of them to death) from the tower of the University of Texas—is more than I find I have the stomach for. These are the crimes that hold the headlines, and yet they are so perverse as to be unlikely to be deterred by any imaginable punishment. The people who committed them either believed they were above and beyond the law, or were incapable of looking beyond the act in any case. Some were undoubtedly mad. But there is a type of killer—Colin Wilson calls him 'the assassin'—for whom murder is not a means to an end, not even as punishment or revenge, but an act of creative expression it itself. Such a killer must have been set on the road to becoming a psychopath early in life, and some never look back: Speck, for example, never bothered to rationalise what he was doing, nor did the English psychopath Neville Heath. But there are clearly others like Manson and Brady who still find some resistance in their minds to the complete indulgence of impulse, and who have to find some intellectual basis for what they do, if only because they like to identify themselves as intellectuals.

What such people are really seeking is power. Usually they are people of strong will but not exceptional intelligence: were they to observe reality and exercise normal reasoning, they would know they are headed for destruction. But having failed already to engage society successfully on its own terms, they must prove themselves right by smashing it. But the only way to do this, since by admission the system has already been fixed, is to resort to a kind of magic, to symbolic actions which work in defiance of reason. Magic is the failure's short-cut to power: anarchist terrorists, revolutionary guerrillas and psychopathic killers all act consciously or unconsciously on this principle. Haigh drinking his victims' blood is an extreme example. Whitman and Oswald shooting *down* from their lofty perches and panicking the smug world below were also making magical gestures to express their secret and unsuspected power. So were the Palestine guerrillas who hijacked airliners and blew them up in the desert. Logically, none of them could achieve anything. Magically—who knows? The psychopath is free from the trammels of causal connection, soaring free above the clouds of doubt.

Compared with Power, Sex is a secondary factor, almost a by-product. From the male point of view (and it is significant that throughout our discussion of violence we are concerned almost exclusively with men) the sexual act is coloured with pleasure, sure enough; but it is an expression both of love and power, and when it comes down to brute rape—of power alone. It can be argued that most hard-core pornography, from de Sade onwards, is more concerned with power than with erection and ejaculation: that the Freudian idea of libido or lust as the central driving force was a false turning, and that the grand high road leads from Schopenhauer and Nietzsche's concept of the Will to the modern ethologist's theories of dominance, identity and territory. Without meaning to be funny, I think we might even take Will back to Shakespeare.

Strictly speaking, though, the true psychopath has no choice to be or not to be anything but what he is. However, there are elements of his make-up in many who retain some freedom of will. Certain societies (notably the United States) come close even to tolerating and encouraging psychopathic behaviour. The emphasis on toughness, action and achievement in the upbringing of young men and boys must bring out violent tendencies; while the restless migration of American families, the frontier tradition of manliness and gun-law, the cultural frictions caused by successive waves of immigration have all made life the harder for those who are mentally and socially maladjusted anyway. It cannot just be due to the more thorough coverage of American news that so many of the classic examples of psychopathic behaviour come from the United States.

What is even more alarming is the deliberate cultivation of psychopathic-style behaviour as a criminal and political technique. It may even have begun as a literary cult, with authors like Hemingway, Raymond Chandler, Ian Fleming—and perhaps we should go back to Nietzsche once again. The American writer Alan Harrington, in his study of Psychopaths[24], refers to the 'revolutionary, hip but also intellectually chic' proposition that compassion is a luxury western Man can no longer afford; that he must replace it with violence, self-assertion and 'combat-readiness' if he wants to survive. From being an illness, psychopathy becomes a conscious military tactic. Madness is cultivated, rehearsed and switched on like a death-ray. It is as if, in order to impress his authority, the usurping emperor calls in the barbarians from the darkness beyond the frontier. They disrupt the law-courts and the colleges, provoke the police, make war on middle-class respectability and nonsense of liberal humanism. 'You believe in tolerance and freedom of expression? Then I express myself freely by shitting on your carpet, pissing on your bookshelves and wiping my arse with your manuscript. Tolerate that!' The veteran Yippie Jerry Rubin, a front-rank and ostentatious eccentric from the Berkeley and Chicago street riots, once proclaimed: 'What we need is a generation of nuisances who are freaky, crazy, irrational, sexy, angry, irreligious, childish and mad!' It was needed, of course, to destroy The System.

But one does not have to take a caricature like Rubin to see deliberate psychopathy at work. The paranoid dream empires of the American Black Muslims were built upon it, and the Black Power movement exploited it even more aggressively— as, indeed, did Hitler's Nazi Party. I never attended a Nazi rally, but I have watched Negro leaders like Stokeley Carmichael, H. Rap Brown and Eldridge Cleaver deliberately throw themselves into convulsions of violent oratory, only to admit later that they had done it simply to stir up the black audience and throw the whites into a guilty panic. The words did not correspond with anything real or probable, 'Any more,' as one of them told me, 'than the words in white advertising copy do.' Cleaver describes how, on leaving jail after a drugs sentence, he declared himself 'mentally free—a law unto myself'—in other words, a psychopath. He set himself the special task of violating the white man's sacred woman. 'I became a rapist,' he writes. 'Rape was an insurrectionary act . . . I wanted to send waves of consternation throughout the white race.' And he quotes an incantation by a fellow Negro, LeRoi Jones:

'Come up black dada nihilismus. Rape the white girls.'

But Cleaver did realise that he was driving himself frantic, cutting himself off from civilised humanity, by deliberately contracting what he calls 'a revolutionary sickness'. Which is a good way of describing this affectation of violence.

The danger is that we shall see much more of this mimicked psychopathy not only in America, but in Britain and all over the western world. It has been familiar to Russians since the days when Dostoievsky wrote of rape and murder as 'fevered expressions of individuality . . . a wish to assert oneself and one's humiliated personality'. There is little real need in the western world today for violence to secure food or shelter: no one seriously embarks upon raids to feed his family. And there is little need now, if there ever was any, for violence purely to indulge a sexual need. What seems to have increased is violence to satisfy rising but disappointed expectations of power. Some of those who resort to such violence are openly and undeniably insane; they give themselves away by the meaningless targets they select. But others are borderline cases who rationalise their violence in terms of politics or class warfare. The assailants of John and Robert Kennedy, Martin Luther King and Governor George Wallace were of that kind. They all felt themselves undervalued and discriminated against, and found theoretical arguments to justify what they did, which had little to do with their underlying resentments.

As education promotes the abler citizen higher and faster than ever, as advertising holds out the same lush prospects to all, and political democracy insists that we are all equal, the less able (though still ambitious) are bound to feel resentment at their failure to achieve what others have achieved. They know what they want to do and they are sure they could do it, given a fair chance—if only the game were not rigged against them and in favour of Teacher's Pets, the people with the right accents. To show how gravely they have been underestimated, how powerful they really are, the rejected minority may resort to violent gestures signalling their message. In one place they will chase the Pakistanis out of a local pub, to keep it white. In another they will start a racket to 'protect' small shopkeepers. Somewhere else again, in Belfast, they will park bombs for the Provisionals, or set themselves up as a Loyalist execution squad. But we shall come to violence among groups in the following chapter.

Here I am concerned with the basic violence of the individual. It is time to round up some conclusions:

We must begin by recognising that Man is by far the most complex of creatures, and that he has made himself a complicated world to live in. Sometimes it is more than he can cope with. And it cannot be denied that some situations, notably those in which he finds himself threatened or thwarted, do trigger a series of chemical reactions which precipitate him towards using force. Yet I believe that Man is not so much violent or aggressive by nature, as exceedingly ambitious. If he were not, he would not be Man. But when it comes to the use of force he is *by nature* remarkably ill-equipped. It is hard to believe that such a soft-handed, slow-footed, blunt-toothed creature could really be classified as, by nature, a killer ape.

Man's instinct to get together in affectionate groups is quite as strong as any instinct to fight off strangers. Man's prime ambition within his group is to assert the personal identity which his society, his family and his peers help him to select from his mental endowment—an endowment which is also influenced by his physical equipment.

The approach to modern Man through apes and cavemen seems to me healthy in jolting us out of undue reverence for our kind: but what we really need to know is more about ourselves as we are. Certainly we resemble other primates in living in groups, with the usual generation gaps and essential differences between male and female roles. We retain a certain instinctive respect for tribal pecking orders, a rather loose sense of territory (which is psychological as much as geographical), and the crumbling remains of certain ritual gestures to avoid violence. But the real trouble with Man is that, thanks to his big brain and perhaps also his varied diet, he has broken away from the limitations of his animal heritage, both bodily and emotional. Man is able to do things which are as 'unnatural' mentally as his bicycling or flying are physically. No mere Naked Ape could have conceived a religion, a political ideology or any generalised abstract idea—let alone have his fellows executed for the Arian Heresy or Leftist Deviation.

More and more, writers about Man are tending to look back wistfully to the Middle Ages. For sure, they produced great cruelty from time to time; but mediaeval churchmen recognised that Man was part beast, part angel, and that it was the function of the angelic soul to tame the beast. In short, they believed in Original Sin; and they would have warned us that it was a delusion to think that Man could be made good simply by placing him in a good environment—restoring him to the Garden of Eden. Abolish the slums, introduce permissive education and free lunches, and you will still get criminal violence in the streets. This mediaeval view of Man is, surely, far more true to experience than the heresy of Rousseau—which indeed goes back to the Renaissance—that Man is not really sinful, that he is essentially good, and that if only our up-bringing and education and laws could be 'natural', Man would be his own God.

I do not really want at this point to begin a long passage on right and wrong. It seems to me that morally prescriptive statements like 'You ought to do X' are really conditional descriptive statements, meaning 'If you were a certain sort of person you *would* do X'. But to cut a long argument short, let 'sinful' mean 'flawed—imperfect'. And what flaws Man is that his reasoning ability to adjust his physical surroundings has far outstripped his hereditary ability to adjust his emotions to the changes he has made. Never mind what we may have been two million years ago: even two hundred years back we were not living in twenty-storey tower blocks, watching American cowboys on a box in our living-room and wondering what the Uganda Asians in the flat above us are cooking for supper.

For the physical changes have come even faster in recent years than the philosophical ones. The revolutionary effects of Man's technology began when Number Eight in the pecking order crept up behind Number One and beat his brains out with an antelope's leg-bone. In 'natural' terms, nothing has quite made sense ever since. Perhaps the really exceptional thing about contemporary violence, and what makes people panicky about it, is the advanced technology of which violent men, like the rest of us, can now avail themselves. Guns are not simply more efficient today, they are mass-produced and everyone can afford them. The gunman can make his getaway in a fast car, hijack an aeroplane and (if thwarted) blow it up with a hand grenade. We may be able to watch it live on TV. Dick Turpin was lucky to hit a Bow Street runner at twenty paces; but who knows how long we shall have to wait before the first crime is committed with the aid of nuclear weapons?

Even so, as Lionel Tiger and Robin Fox observe[52]: there is really no problem of aggression—only the *misuse* of aggression. I have said that I prefer the word 'ambition', partly because it does not carry the implication that violence must follow. What *is* inevitable is that people will strive to make their mark in whatever way seems meaningful to them; and if no other way produces recognition, they may resort to violence.

In this sense, frustration does lead to violence. The frustration may not be as obvious as a simple 'Thou shalt not' from authority, and it may build up over a period of time. It may take the form of lack of opportunity; it may be absence of stimulation, so that the personality has nothing to bring it to life; it may be lack of opposition; it may be sheer boredom; all of these can be frustrating to ambition. It is just as frustrating and conducive to violence to lock up a prisoner in a comfortable bed-sitting-room as to put him in a stone dungeon with bars.

Again, violence is a language, and it may be saying any number of things: 'Help, I can't cope!', 'Give me back my baby!', 'I'm the boss!', 'I *should* be boss!', 'Let me out of here!', 'Go away stranger!', 'I despise women!', 'To Hell with respectability!', and simply 'Get stuffed!', among others. Leaving aside remarkably few cases of intellectualised violence, brutality is a characteristic of the inarticulate, the ignored and the socially backward.

Some readers may have leapt to the conclusion that I would defend the violent criminal on the grounds that the poor fellow had been misunderstood and thwarted by society. 'Why can't the muggers and murderers learn to control themselves like the rest of us?' goes the indignant cry. But there is really no question of defending violent behaviour: it happens, it has happened, it will happen. What are we going to do about it?

As with the question of capital punishment for murder, the conventional reaction to mugging is based on a confusion between the act before it happens, and the act after it has happened. Once violence has taken place the question is how to prevent it happening again—not, what is our instinctive reaction to the thought of it happening? It is even better to ask, how can we prevent such a thing *before* it has happened? In both cases it is a matter of prevention or deterrence, and those who demand tough punishment for violent men claim that this is what they want too. But if they examine their consciences, they will find that what they are really seeking is revenge.

They wish to punish the criminal and make him suffer, not because it will undo the harm done or (necessarily) prevent repetitions, but in order to disidentify themselves with his attitude and actions and purge themselves of any association with him. Such revenge is totally different from deterrence. Christians, surely, ought to have nothing to do with it: they should be trying to cure any sickness or perversion of mind that may have led to violence, and above all trying to prevent any repetition of it. Simply demanding why the violent man did not control himself is futile, unless we genuinely want to know the answer. As a rhetorical question it does nothing but stress the righteousness of those who ask it.

A newspaper lies before me as I write. It headlines the case of a fifteen-year-old boy who killed a five-year-old girl in Coventry. The only explanation he could find for the deed was that his dog had died and he wanted to revenge himself on God. The boy was sentenced to seven years detention; at which, according to my newspaper cuttings, the little girl's father burst out: 'I couldn't believe it—that people can get twenty years for mugging, but for killing a little girl who never hurt anybody, that kid can get off practically scot-free. I don't know how the judge can say that my daughter's life is worth only seven years. I do not know what can be done, but I'm going to explore every avenue.'

It would be unkind to treat this as much more than a cry of grief. One can only pray that time will bring comfort and reason. It may sound fatuous to ask whether the sentence might have been acceptable if the little girl *had* hurt somebody, but it will serve to illuminate the point that no life can ever be priced or paid for in terms of somebody else's suffering. We, as a society, do not fail in punishing the boy too lightly or too harshly, but in allowing his crime to happen in the first place, in allowing him to grow up so tormented that the death of his dog seemed like a conspiracy against him by God. The avenues we need to explore are the pot-holed and overgrown avenues of the human mind. But how we should deal with the violence there, I must leave to my final chapter. I wish now to proceed from the individual to the group.

CHAPTER THREE

The Brotherhood of Violence

THE PROGRESS of violence from individual to group brings two important developments: a change in the scale of violence that becomes possible (leading us to the concept of terrorism), and a real change in its quality, as individual plays upon individual and the total becomes more than the sum of its parts. In particular, violence now demands justification, as members of the group discuss what they are doing and what binds them together. As we have already seen in cases like that of the Manson Family, small groups may adopt some deeply irrational reasons for their deeds; but plausibility is a feature of every successful group, or gang, leader. If the group is clearly identifiable and disliked by outsiders, it is all too easy for it to develop a philosophy of persecution and counter-persecution. In short, with the group comes political violence.

The group is, of course, no recent creation. It is legitimate here to draw parallels between the group organisation of the apes and that of bushmen, aborigines and other less primitive humans. The tribe, the hunting team, the village are natural units of social organisation, and within them are further natural divisions between the elders, the mothers and children and the young braves.

But complications set in once the tribe developed into an even larger unit, the 'supertribe', in which—as Desmond Morris puts it[39]—the individual 'no longer knew personally each member of his community'. Stronger tribes captured the territories of weaker ones and ultimately acquired the allegiance of their inhabitants. Strangers could now walk into our camp claiming to be members of our tribe. If they really wanted to belong, they had to acquire our customs, badges and enemies, but the tribe could never be the same again. The supertribe expanded into the state, the nation.

The nation is a far more efficient machine than the old tribe, for it is big enough and implies sufficient managerial organisation for specialisation and the economies of scale to operate. Sometimes it has grown too big too soon, and bread, circuses, pyramid-building or war have had to be found to occupy the under-employed. Some of the most successful cultures have managed to evolve and freeze rigid social systems in which all uncertainty and friction is eliminated by caste; but this in itself is a confession that, above a certain size, the group has to be broken down into sub-groups if the individual is not to feel threatened with dilution into nothingness. Constantly, however, the sub-group too over-expands, becomes too big, and splinter groups break away from it, each one asserting the identity and importance of its members. But it is worth noting an unexpected paradox here: the splinter group and its leader stand a much better chance in the big city than they do in the small village. For all its reputation as a juggernaut crushing the individual, the city is in fact far more tolerant of non-conformity than the country is.

I believe that the interest we are now seeing in Britain in community politics, in the weakening of party regimentation and the creation of regional assemblies, is an instinctive reaction against the enlargement still further of our 'supertribe': against the giant departments of state, against the replacement of historic boroughs and counties by rationalised administrative units, and against the European Community and its Brussels-based machinery.

As our social units have got bigger, and despite the increasing population, there has not been a proportionate increase in the number of opportunities for leadership. With the spread of mergers and conglomerates, the same is true in business life. Those whose drive to lead is consequently left unsatisfied have a variety of choices: they can lead in some less exalted field, like the Boy Scouts or the local Dramatic Society; they can kick hell out of a football—or even a fellow human-being; or they can found groups of their own, which may increasingly become easier in crime or politics than in business.

In any case, the concentration of power, efficient though

it may be administratively, is bound to leave society with growing numbers of frustrated would-be leaders. They are not necessarily potential cabinet ministers, company chairmen or even county councillors: a generation or two ago such people might have been no more eminent than master-craftsmen or respected leaders of village opinion. The point is, the opportunities for them to assert their importance have gone, although their numbers, education and expectations continue to rise. Some outlet for their ambition has to be found, for these are the leaders and it is leadership that decides what direction a group will move in.

But it is another of Man's characteristics that, thanks to his ability to think in concepts and not just visual images, he is able to carry his admiration (and hatred) from father to father-figure or leader, and from leader to nation, flag, faith or ideology. These last give the individual a feeling of strength. Man does possess a sense of pattern or meaning in life, and for some this becomes religion and the sense of God. In almost everyone there is a need to believe in something that will survive, survive even the fall of the leader; something that the individual shares as the collective faith of his kind, confident that he and fifty million others—or only five others—can't be wrong.

The coup d'état, the overthrow of the established leader by force is by no means unknown in the world of animals. My own cat, an elderly and ponderous Siamese, is fighting desperately at this moment to retain his supremacy over the neighbourhood against the challenge of a newly-arrived and vigorous young tabby tom. But among the animals, as among primitive peoples, such contests are simple matters of territorial Might is Right. The contestants do not claim to be liberating each other, overthrowing false gods or bringing truth to the ignorant. Modern Man, for better or worse, has higher objectives and dares to assume he can devise a future which will, in some sense, be better than the present. In the past he has made some bad miscalculations. There are those who maintain that from (at the latest) 1914 onwards, all change has been for the worse. But that is far too simple a view: however unevenly the gradients of progress may fall and rise, there can be very few people who do not stand higher today than they would have done a hundred, let alone two, three or four hundred years ago. And I have heard too many miners and farm-workers recall the bad old days of their youth to think that even the Edwardian age is to be preferred to our own.

Apparently subversive ideas are not necessarily to be condemned out of hand. So many ideals we now revere were born furtively in small conspiracies. Most of them have encountered repression by authority. Many have had to resort to violence at one time or another in order to triumph or even survive. The advocate of non-violence (which we shall examine in a later chapter) is obliged to ask himself: is he sure that Parliamentary Democracy in Britain, Constitutional Republicanism in America, Independence in Ireland, and Freedom in Bangla Desh, in Greece, in Nazi-occupied Europe could have come about without intellectually justified violence?

It is a good deal easier to find such justification for violence against the occupying foreigner than for violent attempts to overthrow a government of one's own blood. To do that, it is first psychologically necessary to alienate oneself from one's opponent by establishing him as other than, less than, oneself. If he is obviously of the same race and nation, he will have to be locked up in some other category—region, religion, old school, accent, class. Very often the antagonism is mutual and the victim will oblige by adopting some provocative label— which may not actually refer to the real point of difference.

Thus Fascists and Communists are equally nationalistic and totalitarian; but the former persist in harping upon discipline and authority, while the latter pretend to embody the inexorable will of the international proletariat. On a less vicious level, the British Labour Party is not actually inspired by the cause of the Trade Unions at all, but by the consciences of lower middle-class, nonconformist intellectuals; while the Conservative Party, far from conserving the interests of the old ruling class, busies itself carrying out very similar reforms devised by somewhat better-off middle-class leaders who are rather less conscience-ridden and rather more pragmatic. The difference between the two sides is more traditional than real, and both sides, sensing this, find it hard to work up the kind of hatred that could lead to violence. The same is true of the United States, where whatever the causes of violence, they certainly do not include animosity between Republicans and Democrats.

But what if power is monopolised by a single group; or if a two-group, two-party system becomes excessively collusive and unresponsive? Then there is almost bound to be trouble, and it should be worth marking down the conditions under which it may be expected.

At its worst we are talking about Revolution, the violent overthrow not merely of rulers but of the ruling philosophy as well. It should hardly be necessary nowadays to spend much time on the primitive Marxist theory that class conflict makes revolution inevitable; not because Marx was wrong in pointing out the power of technological and economic forces, but because it should be perfectly obvious by now, more than a hundred years after the *Communist Manifesto*, that history is not so simple. Marx grossly underestimated the power of nationalism, the resilience of liberal democracy, the intelligence of capitalism and the conservatism of both workers and peasants. Much of what we now call Communism would be better described as 'the interests and policies of the government in Moscow', and its most faithful ally has been not dialectical conflict but the Red Army.

Nevertheless there *is* economic exploitation, there *are* different social classes, some (though not all) of whose interests are in conflict, and there can be little doubt that everywhere, including the so-called People's Democracies, those with money have more influence over what happens than those without it. But if these were enough to bring about Revolution, there would hardly be a peaceful country in the world. Britain for one— perhaps the most blatantly class-plagued nation in Europe— would have been a howling slaughter-house long ago if inequality alone bred revolt.

Why is it, then, that it does not? American academic research has solemnly formulated, and even expressed in the shape of diagrams, two concepts which may help us to grasp the reasons. Feliks Gross (reporting to the National Commission on the Causes and Prevention of Violence[17]) reckons there are three conditions which must be fulfilled for political violence to take place: conditions of oppression, the existence of a political organisation that believes in direct action, and the

presence of leaders who are personally inclined towards violence. Thus Oppression plus Organisation plus Leadership can
result in Terrorism. Summarised like this, the formula leaves
a good deal still to be explained; but it carries the point that a
number of conditions must come together before anything
happens.

James C. Davies (quoted in another contribution to the
Commission[23]) helps to fill in some of the detail with his
notion of the 'J-curve', in which the J is rotated counter-
clockwise on to its side to represent the gradual rise and sudden
fall of what he calls 'social well-being'. What this means is that
revolutions do not occur (as Marx might have expected) at the
depths of human suffering, nor (as later historians have supposed) when things are getting better. They take place when
conditions have been improving steadily for some time and
then suffer an unexpected setback. T. R. Gurr (of the Commission's staff) comments: 'The greater deprivation an individual perceives relative to his expectations, the greater his
discontent; the more widespread and intense the discontent,
the more likely and severe is civil strife.' Applied to the French
and Russian revolutions, the J-curve theory of expectations
raised by improvement and then frustrated by a sharp setback
rings true.

But we have to be careful here to distinguish between widespread popular revolt (which is rare) and what Gross is really
talking about, terrorism against foreign rule or domestic
dictatorship. Popular revolt and minority terrorism may be
superimposed to reinforce each other; and it is usually the
dream of the terrorist minority to kindle and lead the people's
revolution (whoever 'the people' may be); but the minority is
usually far less representative of the masses than it likes to
pretend. It is specially important for tender-hearted liberals to
be able to recognise when a so-called Liberation group is really
spearheading the suppressed desires of the downtrodden, and
when it is simply the creature of its own ideological fantasies.

A strain of hysterical paranoia in the leadership can rapidly
convince a movement—as it did the Black Power movement in
America during the late 1960s—that a casually unfair society
is consciously malevolent. It is not a question that would go
down well at a protest rally, for protest rallies are not designed

to be reasonable; but the question should be asked at every call to revolt: are things really so bad that only revolution can bring improvement—or are we just bored? And beyond that we should ask whether revolution actually *does* bring improvement, and whether the price is worth paying? The precedents of history are not encouraging.

There may appear to be exceptions: the American Revolution, the Indian Freedom Struggle. But both are better described as transfers of power than as revolutions: there was no turning upside down of the social and economic order in North America, the same gentlemen of property continued to dominate the assemblies; while in India it was the exhaustion by the Second World War, and the votes of the British public, that put spurs to the progress of independence. The real revolution is quite a different matter.

It must begin from a ground of discontent and oppression. Materially, it is not so much a question of absolute deprivation, but of relative disappointment. And the disappointment involves not only the contrast between what was expected yesterday and what was actually achieved today, but between what people had hoped to achieve tomorrow and what they now believe they will get. The greatest disappointment lies in the fear that things will actually get worse; but it is followed closely by the fear that they will not get any better, or at least not reach the level of improvement expected.

If there is working machinery for securing change, a parliament or even a one-party regime with a reputation for responding to the needs and demands of the public, then such fears can be banished or soothed. People may be annoyed from time to time that their hopes have been delayed, but they need not lose faith in their being realised eventually. The belief that change, even dramatic change, can be achieved is very important to a nation's morale; which is why a landslide election victory followed by bold decisions and sweeping legislation are healthy in themselves. It may emerge later that the decisions were the wrong ones and the legislation ineffective; but at least the public feels it has shown itself to possess free will, to be capable of mastering its fate and making changes.

It follows, however, that the relationship between real and expected change needs watching carefully. Politicians really must not continue to offer more than they can fulfil. This is one great advantage that communist regimes enjoy: their control over material conditions of life may be miserly, but it is complete. There is no point in expecting more than you get. The rest of the world may offer a far greater variety of goods and services, but it seems to keep them coming in an uneven flow, and to be unable to match that flow with the expectations aroused by advertising and the mass media. If I were running a totalitarian state, or an underdeveloped nation, I should discourage consumer advertising very severely.

The second ground necessary for violent revolution is political oppression. To some extent this can be provoked or invented: the important thing is that people should *believe* authority to be oppressive, whether it really is or not. Those who are to revolt must be persuaded that the authorities are inflicting unnecessary suffering, enforcing unjust restrictions and discriminating unfairly against particular sections of the community, and that there is no other way of stopping this but by violence.

Beyond the myths and fabrications already being deployed against it, the astonishing thing is that authority so often obliges by making them come true. Time and again (for example, following the 1960s Negro rioting in the United States) commissions of enquiry have found that the forces of law and order have made matters far worse than they need have been, by over-reacting to provocation. Police forces and troops have been so determined to put on an intimidating display of force that the malcontents, as a matter of self-respect if not uncontrollable retaliation, have been obliged to counter-assert their manhood. The authorities then proceed to dispel any remaining respect for law and order by their handling of rioters and people arrested. The enmity is made permanent.

As an immediate example of what I mean, I have before me a dispatch printed in *The Times*, from South Africa, dated October 8, 1973: 'Mr Algy von Holdt, manager of the Western Deep Levels goldmine, where police shot dead 11 black workers on September 11, told the inquest which opened today that there had been no plundering or damage before police arrived on the scene. . . .' (*He said*) 'The whole atmosphere changed

from the time the first shot of teargas was fired by Major
Cloete of the police.'

Revolutionaries desperately need their myths and martyrs.
If the police do not oblige by killing or beating workers, they
must be trapped into doing so. This is the real meaning of the
so-called Politics of Confrontation—to force the other side into
brutality. Tolerant governments must be made intolerant, and
one which persists in trying terrorists as ordinary criminals
under ordinary laws must be panicked—if possible by its own
supporters—into passing special regulations, reviving unusual
penalties and suspending normal civil rights. Then it can be
accused of oppression.

There are, however, two kinds of state where it is very hard
for revolutionary violence to take root. One is the extremely
repressive oligarchy, which may itself have come to power
through revolution, which knows all the tricks and has none
of the scruples. The other is the extremely permissive democracy
which is responsive to the need for change and so is barren as a
field in which to cultivate myths of repression. In such a
society it has to be inconceivable that any activities but the
obviously criminal would be suppressed, or that the police
would use force in any but the most desperate circumstances:
which is one reason why casual beatings by the police are
unforgivable in a country like Britain—such lapses may be
cited some day by enemies of liberty to confirm their alle-
gations that the police are instruments of political oppression.
It is worth putting up with a good deal of provocation, even
with the appearance that the authorities are incapable of controlling a situation, in order to avoid realising the myths which
the would-be destroyers of society require.

If permissive democracy refuses to become oppressive, the
committed revolutionary must still try to find a way of making
it seem so. Ingeniously, the German-American political theo-
rist Herbert Marcuse[32] has offered the theory of 'oppressive
permissiveness', which one might have thought a logical self-
contradiction. It is partly an excuse for the failure of Marxist
prophecies to come true; but it is also the cry of the disappointed
leader who finds that nobody is following him. Abandoning
the dogma that under capitalism the poor must get poorer,
Marcuse grants that increasing material prosperity is actually

part of the system. But by stupefying the masses with false happiness, the system castrates their will and freedom to revolt against it. Free speech is illusory: the liberal Establishment permits such an uproar, such an ideological Tower of Babel, that rival views cancel each other out and only convince the deafened masses that all argument is futile. Therefore the revolutionary minority which (as usual) *knows* it is right must see to it that the uproar ceases and that nothing but the revolutionary truth is heard. In short, Stalin was right—to hell with the dictatorship of the proletariat!

Marcuse, working in way-out California, dreamed of an impossible revolutionary coalition of hippies, students, ghetto blacks and Asian or Latin American guerrillas. At least he was right in saying that the struggle was really between two elites: that in power at present, and the small minority of the supposedly enlightened. The fact is the masses, or as I should prefer to say 'the public', when faced with the question 'Are things so bad that nothing but destruction can set them right?' will almost always reply that things are not *that* bad. There can only be a tiny handful of men and women who are so detached from material possessions, careers and family ties that they are ready to become full-time, committed revolutionaries who must either win everything or lose everything. Ironically, the permissive democracy extends two facilities which make it all the easier for this minority to survive: student grants and social security benefits, though I should be the last to accept this as an argument for restricting either.

To bind itself together, give itself identity and convince itself that it is working for more than selfish ends, the revolutionary band must have a political philosophy. This is relatively simple when the regime it seeks to overthrow is a foreign one, or can be personified in a single autocrat who has to be replaced. That was the case with almost all violent conspiracies up to the French Revolution. But justification becomes more difficult when the regime already has some claim to represent the public interest, when it is a whole system and way of life that has to be torn down, when people have to be persuaded to accept not merely a new king but a whole new social and political order. And when that order is quite capable of reforming itself without revolution (though not, perhaps, of making those reforms required by the revolutionaries in their own interests) then the need for myths and demons becomes pressing. Their one great advantage is that they simplify impenetrably complex situations and so convince people they have found the truth. This is a human characteristic upon which tyrants have always been able to play: we all desire to understand the situations in which we find ourselves, it is difficult to understand their true complexity, but we seize gratefully at a simple explanation not because it is accurate, but because at last here is something we can grasp. The simplicity of polytheism, of God-and-the-Devil, of witchcraft, of Racism, of Materialism, have been successively their great appeal. It is far easier to explain away apparent contradictions to any of them than to construct an objective explanation of what is in question.

Fundamental to all rationalisation of group violence there must be this simple commitment to unreasoning force—to terror, if not ultimately to open civil war. Terrorists commonly insist that those who do not join them are the cowed victims of the very oppression they are fighting, yet they also insist that (in the words of the French anarchist bomber of the 1890s) 'there is no such person as the innocent bystander'. Violence is supposed to make us take sides. It has also been worshipped as the only really pure, clean form of action, having a beauty in its own right regardless of motive or consequence. This I suspect is just another form of escapist over-simplification. Violence is a psychological relief and release, especially for people whose restrained words and actions seem to have won them neither results nor respect.

Terror brings the additional satisfaction of making the enemy look deflated and ridiculous. 'The Terrorist Party', wrote the Russian theoretician Morozov, 'must push without mercy a programme of continuous terror to punish the government and render it powerless;' and the party, which never numbered more than about five hundred, held earnest discussions about random terror, 'focussed terror' and mass terror. For more than thirty years from the 1880s, terror became a whole style of politics in Russia, spreading outwards into Poland, the Balkans and the Austro-Hungarian and Turkish Empires.

It is debatable whether modern terrorism really began in Russia, or in Ireland with the Republican Brotherhood and the

Fenians (who conducted Britain's first bomb outrages while Queen Victoria was still on the throne). The Irish might claim to be first on the scene, in the 1840s or even earlier: they were neck-and-neck with the Russians in exploiting the infernal machine. But there is always something inward-looking about Irish movements: Fenianism was essentially a patriotic gesture against the foreign ruler, whereas nineteenth-century Russian Terrorism developed into a much deeper philosophy, an intellectual substitute for the old fervour of religion. Yet the Russian terrorists first saw violence as a weapon that would-be social democrats were obliged in their circumstances to use against tyranny—as a weapon that was not legitimate in a free democracy like America. Prior to the Revolution, neither the Bolsheviks nor the Mensheviks really approved of it.

But as early as 1871, in *The Possessed*, Dostoievsky had had a vision of what the revolutionary elite would do when they came to power:

'First we must enforce obedience . . . everything will be reduced to a common denominator, complete equality will be enforced. . . . Occasionally, however, every thirty years or so, we will let them have a shock; and then they will all suddenly begin to devour each other. Of course we'll only let it reach a certain point, just to stave off boredom.' Could there have been a better forecast of Maoist communism and the Cultural Revolution?

Revolutionaries like Dostoievsky's Shigalev are obliged to use violence for two reasons: first, to dislodge the existing regime, and second, to ensure that the public which has thus been liberated is terrorised into accepting the revolutionary version of freedom. As René Fülop-Miller says in his monumental work on Bolshevism[20] the new truth is that humanity can only be made happy by compulsion, by being deprived of the intolerable burden of freedom and taught that the only way to happiness is through absolute obedience. This, surely, is the essence of the Jesuit method. It came to communism from the Jesuits, by way not of Marx but the nihilists like Bakunin.

'Freedom', declared Lenin, 'is a bourgeois prejudice. We repudiate all morality which proceeds from supernatural ideas or ideas which are outside class conceptions. In our opinion morality is entirely subordinate to the interests of the class war. Everything is moral which is necessary for the annihilation of the old exploiting social order and for uniting the proletariat. Our morality consists solely in close discipline and conscious warfare against the exploiters.'

So morals are nothing but weapons in the class war, dictated by economic interests. And when those interests are overthrown, morals too must change. The end justifies the means, even if those means involve worse brutality than that employed by the oppressors.

Whole-hearted terrorism is only possible in the long run for people who are psychopathically inclined. Many violent revolutionaries have begun as idealists, only to become sickened at the depths of cruelty to which their work drags them in the end. But revolutions are besotted with the dream of making everyone not only happy and free but virtuous: what corrupts them, says Camus, is the substitution of Virtue for Love.

A government becomes oppressive, incompetent and corrupt. Terrorism weakens it still further; it loses its grip on the armed forces and the revolution triumphs. At first a coalition takes office; but the left becomes impatient with compromise and turns upon 'the enemies of the Revolution'—which is to say, anyone not enthusiastically in favour of the leftist view. The right and the centre are liquidated in a Thermidorean reign of terror. The people *shall* be virtuous; they must demonstrate their enthusiasm for the new virtues by demonstrating against the old vices and lynching the former heroes of the Liberation and the Resistance, who by now are paralysed with horror at what their struggle has led to. In the end the reaction comes: Cromwell or Buonaparte or Lenin steps in, and the left in its turn is crushed. The pragmatic hero takes over and a new, drab bureaucracy is established.

The cycle has been repeated again and again. At the root of it all lies Rousseau's Romantic Fallacy, that Man is born Good, and that he is only corrupted by private property and by the state which has been created to protect it. The doctrine seems to me so naive, inadequate and shallowly self-fulfilling that Original Sin (against which it was a natural reaction) is far closer to the mark, for all its weaknesses. So long as the christian tradition was strong, western society was resistant to the idea that Man's Good was a matter for political definition. But secular thinkers like Marx and Engels were easy converts to Original Virtue. What they did not seem to recognise or care about was that, despite its origins in the Romantic Movement, the passion to enforce the natural goodness in Man could only achieve its aims through violence and not through love. In short, it led straight to terror.

And the ultimate perfection of terror was Nazi Germany, where cruelty became the official instrument of state policy, made easier to wield by the complete alienation and degradation of its victims. This brings us now to the German contribution to the philosophy of violence.

The wars and terrors of the French Revolution, which Rousseau had innocently helped to inspire, left their reaction. Philosophers like Gobineau and Schopenhauer declared Man to be 'the ultimate wild beast'—'in no way less cruel and pitiless than the tiger and the hyena'. Worse than bestial, Man was diabolical: he alone inflicted pain not just to satisfy hunger or in the fury of battle, but for its own sake. Man's criminal record, wrote the gloomy Schopenhauer, flowed from his inborn nature, his colossal egoism, his blind, predestined Will. Man must be what he is; he is what he does; and what he does is the result of that fixed and unalterable inner Will. Intellect is mere rationalisation. The only escape is through quietism or suicide.

But not everyone was so appalled by what the Revolutionary wars had shown Man to be capable off. During the 1820s, Hegel was lecturing at Berlin on the Philosophy of History, and saw the 'colossal egoism' of men like Napoleon, Julius Caesar and Alexander the Great as carrying out the Will of the World Spirit. These, Hegel said, were practical men of action who had sensed the principle behind events, had realised what the world was ready for, and promoted it ruthlessly. As for the suffering they inflicted on the way, individual morality could not be allowed to stand in the way of the World Spirit. The mighty feet of History on the march must trample many an innocent flower.

Despite the fact that Schopenhauer detested the vulgarity of Hegel's philosophy, they had a good deal in common: the inevitability of cruelty, the obedience of the individual to his destiny, the minor role played by reason in pursuing that destiny. Hitler, one of the most dangerous self-educators and simplifiers in history, read everything he could lay hands on in his search for confirmation of his crude *Weltanschauung*[70]; and he found much of it in Hegel and Schopenhauer, along with Clausewitz, Treitschke and Nietzsche. We know that Nietzsche was on Hitler's bookshelves, though oddly enough Hitler paid no explicit tribute to him in his speeches or writings.

But Nietzsche is really the flower of that tree that bore Hitler as its fruit. His *Twilight of the Idols*[42] and *The Anti-Christ*[42] are fundamental texts for the study of modern violence. Nietzsche denies that there is any valid foundation for morality. As for 'free will', it is a trap set by the churches to make Man accountable for his actions, merely in order to make him guilty of sin. There is *no* metaphysical purpose in life: the denial of God is the greatest freedom. What is Good? Certainly not the unselfishness of Christian manners, for that is pure self-destruction. The Good is everything that heightens the feeling of power in Man, the will to power and power itself. The Bad is all forms of weakness.

Nietzsche exalts Schopenhauer's Will to Survive. He was not, however, impressed by Darwin and the Survival of the Fittest. He complained that the weak in body were often superior in mind, and that the 'fittest' were too often defeated only because they were outnumbered and outwitted. Progress was by no means inevitable. The nineteenth-century European Nietzsche thought greatly inferior to Renaissance Man.

Reaching back to Hegel, Nietzsche conjured up a higher type of man, the Superman. Entire nations might aspire to Superman status, but christianity (with its worship of the weak) had constantly sought to undermine such beings by preaching pity, meekness and forgiveness. It had debauched the intellect of Man by inventing the entire system of natural values. See how the churches had destroyed the noble Roman Empire from within, how they had denied an emasculated Europe the virile influences of Islam! Nietzsche was profoundly anti-semitic and rabidly Teutonic. He saw Christianity as a Jewish trick to survive at all costs. 'How a German could ever have felt Christian is beyond me!' he wrote. 'If Europe never gets rid of Christianity, the Germans will be to blame.' And then, in a paroxysm of hatred almost unmatched in philosophy: 'I condemn Christianity on the most terrible charge any prosecutor has ever made. . . . The Church has left nothing untouched by its depravity, it has made a lie of every truth.'

This worship of power, this hatred of gentleness, pointed towards one great climax in life: War. 'When one renounces War,' Nietzsche declared, 'one renounces life on the grand scale.' War was the one true experience of freedom, of assuming the entire responsibility for the pursuit of one's own advantage. In battle, the manly instincts that delighted in power at last asserted their supremacy over the instinct for mere happiness. And Nietzsche pointed out something that many violent revolutionaries have found to be true: that the value of the struggle lies in itself, not in the achievement of the freedom which is said to be the objective. For once democratic liberal freedoms have been secured, they proceed (says Nietzsche) to reduce everyone to the same smug, cowardly level. There is no longer any room for Superman.

Because leadership, and the pecking order of leadership, is so important to militant groups, this analysis is of even greater importance in civil and guerrilla warfare than it is in wars between nations. It is even harder to make peace with terrorists than it is with foreign governments, because once peace is restored the terrorist loses his stage, his profession, his entire way of life. The most extreme example of this is the late Che Guevara[65], who abandoned liberated Cuba, first to train black guerrillas in the Congo (an experience he found disappointing and at times sickening) and then to lose his life in a futile campaign in Bolivia.

What has canonised Che among guerrillas is that unlike most revolutionary theorists he actually practised what he preached. He was a Hemingway-esque action intellectual, and I cannot help feeling that with Che the Spanish pride in *machismo* ('manliness' of a special kind) always came before Marxism. Guevara had a highly developed theory of how the guerrilla war should evolve and be conducted; but he insisted that he had never even read the works of Mao on the subject—that his theories were drawn from his own first-hand experience entirely. Thus he had no use for centralised party discipline, or for the classic communist formula in which the revolution begins with strikes

by the industrial workers. Che considered the urban proletariat too soft and too much under the thumb of authority.
Nor need one wait for the classic 'revolutionary situation' to
develop: with enough conviction in his heart, and enough
dedication to the cause of the peasants, the guerrilla could go
out and start the revolution *now*, almost anywhere. Once create
a focus, and revolution, like fire, will dry out the surrounding
country and feed itself. The countryside is the proper battlefield, for there a picked band can gradually create its own
legend and win the confidence of the peasantry while undermining the dignity of the government.

Guevara's writings are full of useful tips about clothing and
equipment, about sex on the battlefield, the type of engagements to be fought and avoided, how to collect intelligence,
how to get publicity and when to move from one phase of the
campaign to the next. Running through it all is an infatuation
with the heroic life of the guerrilla as an ideal in its own right:
small wonder that Che in peacetime eventually became fed up
with his duties as an economic planner and turned back to the
hills and jungles once more, choosing death rather than
bureaucracy.

Parallel with Che Guevara's, though a good deal less
physical, lies the career of another philosopher of contemporary
violence: Frantz Fanon[64], a black French psychiatrist from
Martinique who is one of the prophets of the Black Power
movement. Fanon brought to revolutionary theory the rage
and passion of the victims of two phenomena which the nineteenth century had largely taken for granted: colonialism and
racism. The Second World War had taught subject races from
Singapore to Morocco that the white powers were not invin-
cible, and it was in the interests of the communist party everywhere to develop the theme. To do them justice, the colonial
powers themselves were trying to shed the load by transferring
power to brown, black and yellow Englishmen and Frenchmen,
but one result of this was to bring their trainees into closer
contact with European revolutionary teachings. It also emphasised the gap between the native peoples and their culture and
those of the imperial homelands.

The feeling that black people had—or *had* had—a rich,
proud and militant culture of their own really began among

the ex-slaves of the United States, with W. E. B. Du Bois'
Niagara Movement, founded in 1905, with Marcus Garvey's
Universal Negro Improvement Association and with the early
Black Muslim sects that grew up during and shortly after the
First World War. The success of pseudo-Islamic notions
among the Negroes is interesting, for Islam was obviously
accepted as a faith which was non-white, had a tradition of
military violence, and was known to have defeated the churches
of the West.

Fanon, though not in any sense Islamic, did bring together
the slave heritage of the Caribbean and Muslim pride of
North Africa. The turning point of his career was his experience
as a psychiatrist in an Algerian hospital of what torture could
do both to its victims and its practitioners. He became convinced that torture was being used by the French less to gain
information than to satisfy their sadistic racism: that the
opportunity to commit atrocities against black people was one
of the motives behind colonialism. Fanon came to the conclusion that so violent a system could only be removed by
violence. But more than that: it was absolutely necessary for a
colonial people to pass through the refining flames of violence
in order to define its identity and commit itself irrevocably to
true independence. Freedom had to be seized, not granted.
After terror, assassination and bloodshed had driven the two
sides apart, there could be no question of gentlemanly compromise.

For Fanon despised middle-class nationalist parties like the
Indian National Congress which stooped to negotiate freedom
with the imperial slave-masters. National liberation must be
taken out of the hands of the half-white bourgeoisie. Even the
native city workers were no better, for they too had com-
promised with imperialist culture and business, had become a
nation of waiters and taxi-drivers. As for the Russian myth of
the coalition of workers and peasants, it was meaningless for
the bulk of the Third World.

Nor had Fanon much respect for the autocratic revolutions
conducted by men like Lumumba in the Congo and Nkrumah
in Ghana. The only honest revolution was the peasant uprising, aided perhaps by the lowest of the urban low, the petty
criminals, hustlers and prostitutes who had been rejected by

the system. But any outsider who wanted to join the revolt
must realise that he had been cut off intellectually from the
people; he must go back to the villages and let the peasants re-
educate him. Playing with Europeanised power only led to the
kind of parody which Fanon described in his book *The Wretched
of the Earth*:

'Scandals are legion, ministers enrich themselves, their wives
dress themselves up, MPs feather their nests, and there is not
a soul down to the policeman on the beat or the customs
officer who does not leap aboard the bandwagon of corruption.'

Fanon's theories appalled the academic revolutionaries of
the Moscow school, who had to insist (out of self-justification)
that the peasants would always need the leadership of city-born
agitators and intellectuals. Fanon himself was an odd specimen
to be extolling the virtues of the simple peasant. He knew very
little of African life and culture, possessed a thoroughly Frenchi-
fied mind and owed far more to Sorel and Sartre than he did
to any tribal wisdom. And whereas the old Marxists treated
violence as a practical, tactical weapon, Fanon wrote of it as
something existential and almost religious. At the same time I
cannot help suspecting that he also saw it as a means of inflam-
ing the apathetic masses so that they would be in the mood to
follow intellectual leaders like himself. That is how I interpret
the following passage: 'Violence alone, violence committed by
the people, violence educated and organised by its leaders,
makes it possible for the masses to understand social truths and
gives the key to those social truths. . . . Violence on a national
scale liquidates tribalism and regionalism while binding the
community together and committing each individual in the
eyes of himself and others.'

These, then, are the main streams of thought which are now
invoked to justify the violence of the group. Some contradict
others, but all are available to satisfy the demand for shape and
meaning to events which a leader must be able to supply for
his followers. The important thing about revolutionary theory
is not that it should be accurate or objective: what is demanded
is a simple pattern of thought which will take in and justify
the salient myths and martyrs of the group, putting heroes in
the right, villains in the wrong, and meeting the subjective

demand of the rank and file to know they are the servants of what is just and inevitable.

Beyond particular complaints of oppression or injustice certain themes recur. The christian religion is an invariable enemy, not just because it has become identified with the ruling classes and their property values (something the churches should have considered long ago as a serious impediment to their mission), but also because christianity has always been seen by outsiders as encouraging physical and intellectual subservience, even cowardice. It is not, in short, a manly religion to most revolutionaries. Napoleon considered it vastly inferior to Islam. I have already quoted enough of Nietzsche on 'Christianity—the metaphysics of the hangman'. Schopenhauer had one of his characters declare that while Religion might be a good way of taming and training the wickedness of the human animal, a fraud, however pious, was still a fraud: princes used God as a bogy to frighten the children into bed. And Winwood Reade concludes his *magnum opus:* 'Christianity must be destroyed. . . . Not only the Syrian superstition must be attacked, but also the belief in a personal God, which engenders a slavish and Oriental condition of the mind; and the belief in a posthumous reward, which engenders a selfish and solitary condition of the heart.'

But, as we have seen above, there is an equally strong suspicion of Reason, which is dismissed as serving only to justify the repressiveness of those in authority. After all (it is argued) who lays down the rules of the reasoning game? The professors and teachers appointed by Authority to bring up the young in its ways. Professor John Searle[46] writes of the 'flight from Reason' in western industrial societies, and observes how student revolutionaries commonly seek to find some sacred ideal which is, by definition, unchallengeable and 'non-negotiable'. It follows that the enemy of the student radical is whoever will not fall down and worship his sacred cow.

Even so it is hard to prevent futile argument from clogging the wheels of the revolutionary movement. Only violence is pure and uncompromising, expressing the commitment and responsibility of every individual. Violence is not merely a means towards liberation, it is a liberating experience in itself, just as power is felt to be good in itself, for it realises the purpose of Man which is to act, not to argue. Thus War is beautiful—it is really living, even for a Japanese suicide pilot. What is bad is weakness, the refusal of violent action.

The further away the theorists move from sophisticated Western Europe, with its disillusioning experience of popular participation, the more they seem to drift back to the dream that somewhere, out in the countryside, simple working property-less people are inherently good, or at least free from vice. The trouble with the People in general is that too many of them have become corrupted by the industrial purposes of the cities and become dupes or agents of the capitalist ruling classes. Nevertheless, if only the People could be made to recognise and enforce their own true interests, they would be free and virtuous once more. A short cut to this is to make virtue and freedom, as defined by the revolutionary elite, compulsory.

As society becomes more complex in organisation and technology—a process which feeds upon itself and is spurred on by the growth of population and by the sheer joy of command experienced by the managerial elite—the revolutionaries have found to their astonishment that their opportunities have become not less but greater. The communications media, while quite properly reporting the activities of the rebels and drawing attention to the grievances they represent, can serve to magnify their importance and to consolidate the forces of the aggrieved. Modern weapons technology has placed devastatingly effective tools in the hands even of amateurs. And in an age of recent world wars and citizen armies, there are many who are not amateurs. The techniques of one revolutionary movement are speedily communicated to another: the hideous Ulster car-bomb, in which the everyday vehicle becomes the shrapnel, was invented by the Viet Minh in Indo-China, where it had its modest beginnings in the bicycle-bomb. I have seen what a bicycle with a claymore mine lashed inside the frame can do to a crowded vegetable market: it makes all reason look fatuous, and blood the one truth.

Again, the targets that present themselves in developed countries—the aircraft, crowded buildings, communications centres and public services—are a great deal more vulnerable and expensive than anything that (for example) John Brown was able to seize at Harper's Ferry. And once more, the media of publicity can turn the smallest gesture of defiance into a symbolic ceremony of worldwide renown. If the other side has a bad conscience, or is tender-hearted towards human life, it may very well give way. Still more important, the proliferation of disruptive incidents may make it lose confidence and authority, strain its material resources to breaking point, and finally lead the government's own supporters to withdraw their mandate. An important revolutionary propaganda technique is to squeeze up the time-scale within which the public expects the authorities to produce results, so that patience is believed to be running out much sooner than it need do.

In Ireland, in Palestine, in Cyprus, Aden, Algeria, Vietnam and Cuba such methods have claimed their successes, and I am not here concerned with whether the causes behind them were morally justified or not. The mythology is now firmly established that such methods can succeed still further, that 'unacceptable levels of violence' can force systems to surrender, even in situations where orthodox Marxist dialectics indicate that they should not. It is very largely psychological warfare from within—far more disturbing than assaults from without—and no one stands more to lose from the growth of such independent terrorism than the communist establishments of Eastern Europe and China.

Disillusionment with the respectability of Moscow has driven a good many young activists into mimicking the outrageous behaviour of the psychopath, behaviour which makes no sense in orthodox revolutionary terms but only as gratuitous, irrational gestures designed to break through the sheer boredom of everyday existence and assert the existence of the activist. This is existential violence, and Sartre saw it as an attempt to escape from the role of victim in which so many people find themselves cast, to become the subject of one's own existence instead of a mere object. Kidnappings, sky-jackings, bank robberies and car-bombings have no place at all in orthodox Leninist tactics. They are ways of telling Lenin to move over.

But they are also ways of deflating the bourgeoisie, the middle-class herd which the ruling class has virtually invented to take the place of the proletariat. The revolutionary has always known the secret weakness of the bourgeois citizen: that he is terribly afraid of pain and highly susceptible to systematic violence. He expects other people to play fair and not hit below the belt, and he panics when he finds himself in a fight with no rules. A key moment in the life of every revolutionary is when he experiences pain and finds that he can survive it, even learn from it. His middle-class opponent who has been shielded from violence all his life will surrender sooner than learn the same lesson.

It is questionable, though, whether a society which is accustomed to violence is any better off than a soft one like Britain. Authority likes to believe that violence does not pay, yet the history of the United States is a long series of violent episodes many of which *have* paid. At the least, it is a chain of clashes between people demanding change and people insisting on the status quo, and as the Skolnik Report[47] observes, to resist necessary change and stand pat on Law and Order is to leave little alternative to violence. Skolnik remarks gloomily that commission after commission, from the one that investigated the Chicago riots in 1919, through the Harlem Commission of 1935 on to the Kerner Commission of 1968 saw its recommendations on the improvement of police operations accepted, and its suggestions for social reform ignored.

For all that I have said about the justification of political violence by clever theorists, it still remains the case that most outbreaks are the result of a breakdown in the machinery for adjusting society. From the Jacquerie of 1358, the rebellion of Wat Tyler in 1381, the German Peasant revolt of 1525 and the Pilgrimage of Grace in 1536, and on into the eighteenth century there has always been a half-acknowledged right of the people to revolt when that machinery fails. The spread of the national police force during the nineteenth century and the flow of population from the countryside of Europe and America into the cities seem to have changed the whole character of popular protest into something far more intellectual and conspiratorial.

The civil violence of America—and some would say the personal violence underlying it—deserves in my view a word of special explanation. There has never been any other country remotely like America—a country whose population has been almost entirely imported, and from widely varied sources and cultures over a remarkably short span of time. Nor has there ever been a country with such temptations, such demands for high achievement, such contempt for failure. With all these strains and stresses has come an explosion of affluence, education and technology of every kind. Social and geographical mobility, the chance to climb, the chance to move on, have torn people up from their roots and pitched them into a whirlwind of frantic competition.

To a large degree, American violence is the result of throwing together successive waves of immigration, all of them fighting for places in society which will make them feel wanted and important. No nation has ever had to absorb so varied and seething a banquet of humanity, or to go through the simultaneous experiences of pregnancy, delivery, adolescence and indigestion.

America's biggest single digestive problem has been one too long postponed: how to permit the Negro people, imported like cattle over a period of three hundred years and deliberately deprived of their own social and cultural pride, to join a white society as if they had just stepped off the boat like any other immigrants. On both sides, the prejudices and bitterness of three centuries has made this almost impossible. The American immigrant has always stood sure of his identity as an Irish-American, an Italian-American, a Polish-American or even a White Anglo-Saxon Protestant American. The African tribal system gave people an equally clear identity within the group; but slavery had deliberately set out to shatter that. So behind America's black riots has lain not only the frustrations of a group unjustly discriminated against, but the search of a people without a history for battles and heroes of its own.

Much the same questing is to be found in most rebel groups, however brutal and psychotic they may seem to their opponents. Whether they are the Zionist Stern Gang, the Greek Cypriot EOKA, the Kenyan Mau Mau, the Algerian FLN, the Irish Republican Army, the Angry Brigade, the Uruguayan Tupamaros, the American Black Panthers, the Palestinian Black Septembrists or the Front Libre Quebecois, the dedication to violence is in strong part a substitute for religion. The hijackings and the bombings are also signs that a generation which is far better educated than ever before and has been exposed to all the most stimulating theories of the age is still starved of emotional satisfaction, of what in days gone by would have been religious nourishment.

That is one disastrous defect to be discussed in my final chapter, that we have become, in Ardrey's words, 'a species without a religion'. Although we have every reason for needing one, we have no sense of common destiny, no sense of being brothers and sisters under the fatherhood of God or anything else. The more that sense is dispersed, the easier it is for the violent sub-group in search of an identity to achieve one by alienating its brothers and sisters as strangers, even though they may speak the same language. By living apart, schooling apart, marrying apart, false 'foreign languages' can be created and communication shut off. Once that is achieved, the stranger can become an enemy and violence can legitimately be used against him. Fighting lifts us out of a drab and boring existence and identifies us with action, suffering, glory. There is no more dreadful example of this than Ulster.

Ulster has had very little need of intellectual myths to justify violence: it has a long and bitter folk memory, and violence has always supplied that memory with graphic images, has rammed the people into their immutable moulds. As the New Ulster Movement remarked in a striking pamphlet on 'Violence and Northern Ireland', when a man there is killed for political or social reasons, he has been sentenced to execution for the crime of being the only kind of person he knew how to be. There can be no reasoning about this: increasingly, in a violent situation, people will listen only to their own arguments; and they argue that since reason has patently failed, the only answer is counter-violence. Among other things, this offers a devil-sent outlet for the aggressive, anti-social young men who hang about in every dead-end society looking for power and importance.

And so it happens that Thomas Madden was stabbed to death with 150 thrusts as he hung from the ceiling; and David McClenaghan, a mongol boy of fifteen who was forced to witness the rape of his mother, and then was shot to death as the ravished woman tried to shield him. There could be no calculation here that violence would in any way improve things:

it was simply the easiest answer to the question: 'Who am I in this situation of brute force?' The whole history of Ulster for the past seventy years and more bears witness to the self-perpetuating non-solution of violence. To answer force with force becomes more and more a defining act of pride. The opposing side appears less and less human—and, indeed, both sides behave less and less like human beings, making that process easier. The professional killer—who may be good for little else—gains an acknowledged perch on the social tree. People are caught up in the spiral of violence without understanding its causes. One Protestant woman wrote: 'I no longer have any compassion for any nationalist, man, woman or child. After years of destruction, murder, intimidation, I have been driven against my better feelings to the decision—it's them or us.'

CHAPTER FOUR

The Lords of Violence

THE FEELING that 'It's them or us—we must kill or be killed' is one of the psychological flywheels that keep war going. Another is the fact that, most of the time, War is Fun. That is shocking but true—just as it is true that, at certain moments, a man *must* kill or be killed. When the battle is over and the cost of victory or defeat lies rotting on the ground, a disillusioned general may confess (as Sherman probably did *not*), 'War is Hell'; but in the excitement of action, which is what matters, men have always found war a stimulating and liberating experience. It is one of the paradoxes of our civilisation that the state, one of whose social purposes is to eliminate or suppress violence between individuals and violence between groups, finds itself the master of frustrated energies and loyalties all too eager to find release in violence against other states—almost regardless of the consequences. How else can one explain man's persistent failure to see that he would be better off *not* going to war?

War identifies the uprooted, bewildered individual with his soldierly role, with his unit and with his country. For the leader, war is the supreme managerial opportunity, compared with which running a business or a government department is a tedious rigmarole. At war, the entire resources of the nation are available to be deployed on the grandest scale. Bold imagination can be realised with breathtaking impact. The most fundamental of human instincts can be appealed to without embarrassment, the noblest of human emotions be called forth, and the finest attributes of courage, loyalty, sacrifice and comradeship be relied upon with a certainty sadly lacking in the selfish days of peace. At last the nation is a family of brothers again; social divisions fade away. Orders are obeyed without question—or, if they are questioned, the objections can be dismissed as faint-hearted. All of a sudden, life becomes simple and clean. Its cluttering complications are cut away at a blow, and the soldiers of both sides roll honestly towards the battlefield, waving and cheering at the cameras, the sides of their lorries painted 'Cairo (or Tel Aviv) Express', 'Hanoi (or Saigon) here we come', 'Berlin (or Paris) or Bust'. Only after the armies have clashed come the pictures of the dead, mutilated and captured; and those pictures usually present the casualties of one side for the satisfaction of the other. It is unpatriotic to reveal one's own men in a state of shell shock or clutching an armful of guts. Has any radio or television news programme ever brought its audience the sound of the wounded in no-man's land, crying all night for help? That would be the facts, straight and without comment.

Is there any difference, though, between the violence of war, the violence of revolution and the violence of individual murder? Clearly civilisations have always brought up their citizens to believe so, and for reasons which should be familiar by now. A society which will hang a murderer for killing his neighbour will decorate a sergeant for machine-gunning a dozen foreigners in the interests of the state; just as revolutionaries will insist that assassinating a minister for political reasons is totally different from poisoning one's mother-in-law.

In a work which I suspect is only half satirical[26] Edward Hyams actually proposed that assassination could be employed as a useful substitute for war. After all, he argued, it was the statesmen who were responsible for war, why should they not suffer the ultimate consequences of it? Indeed, anthropologically and morally speaking, we might be entitled to sacrifice those rulers who represented the evil in our public life. Did not St Thomas Aquinas hold that the individual had the right, based upon the same natural law that humanists cite, to resist tyranny, even to the extent of assassination for the public good? And who could doubt that it would have been entirely beneficial to the world, had Hitler, Mussolini and Stalin been assassinated long before their armies had begun marching across their frontiers? Terrorism and assassination are far more sparing of life than full-scale war. Even car-bombing takes

fewer lives than bombing from the air. How can we grudge a
few dozen lives a year, maybe, when the 1940 Luftwaffe raids
on Rotterdam took 980, the Blitz on London 13,000, the 1943
Royal Air Force firestorm over Hamburg 40,000, the Nagasaki
Atom Bomb 39,000, the Hiroshima Bomb 75,000, the American
fire-raid on Tokyo 83,000 and the RAF raids on Dresden
135,000? Where is our sense of perspective?

Hyams's modest proposal has considerable charm, though I
fear it would not work. Even if states as a whole could be persuaded to adopt this kind of symbolic warfare, the most evil
men are invariably the best protected. The forces required to
eliminate them would grow in size until there was no difference
between the attempt to kill off the dictator and the struggle to
destroy his defence force—which is virtually what the Second
World War was anyway. If the suggestion is that public-
spirited freelances should lay down their lives picking off the
tyrants before they go too far, then indeed it is already being
attempted—and guarded against. We shall never know what
the world has been saved by the assassinations which have
succeeded: would John F. Kennedy really have saved America
from the blood-letting of Vietnam? But apart from the mentally disturbed, those who kill our rulers are seldom content to
stand modestly back and let the public decide what comes next.
They usually have their own firm ideas of what is good for the
newly-liberated.

In any case, war by assassination would deprive nations of
the excitement that warriors feel as they prepare for battle. It
would cheat us of our fun, and maybe a of good deal more.
Yet another semi-satirical work of genius (Leonard Lewin's
Report from Iron Mountain[28]) sardonically observes that 'the
war system' is in fact the real driving force behind our social
organisation. It clarifies issues (because there can only be two
sides to any war), it provides a flywheel for industrial production and employment, it dissipates boredom, provides periodic opportunities to adjust the moral code, while still enabling
the ruling older generation to maintain its hold over the
fighting younger generation. War, says Lewin (who disguises
himself as a mythical presidential commission), is not the
servant or product of our social system, it moulds that system.
Even though it does not have to break out very often, its

possibility is an end in itself. The government's emergency war powers are what really keeps a society together.

There is far too much truth in this to be comfortable. Lewin would argue that a bungled, incomplete war like Vietnam is a mockery of the true war system—almost worse than none at all; but with Vietnam out of the way, his thesis is coming into its own again. Although he is writing primarily of the United States, much of what he says rings true of Britain during the Second World War. I have had more recent, first-hand experience of the tonic effect a 'good' war can have upon a depressed people: the Bangla Desh War of December 1971 between India and Pakistan. After more than twenty years of disappointing independence, of more talk than achievement, of running hard to stay in the same place, and of watching the nation's international importance steadily decline, India finally did something right. There was a great deal of hypocrisy and dirty work about the way in which the war was helped to break out. The armed forces of both countries were eager to have a bash; the peoples were fired with indignation. From India's point of view there was a good cause to support beyond the perennial one of helping Pakistan on her way to perdition: that of establishing the independence of the Bengalis—or at least of the eastern, muslim Bengalis. The Indian Army did the right things in the right places at the right time (the Pakistanis did all the wrong things); it fought efficiently and decisively, and it achieved the desired result with the minimum of damage and casualties. It was, perhaps, the last of the gentleman's wars, a bloody good show without too much bloodshed, and almost everyone (except the Pakistanis) felt the better for it. Even the Pakistanis may secretly have been relieved to lose the Bengalis—in the face of superior force. A couple of years later, Indian national morale was back in the dumps, but at least Bangla Desh was surviving as a parliamentary democracy. So, seeing that those involved were apparently prepared to pay the price, how can anyone condemn the war as totally evil? Evils there certainly were, but on balance surely it was justified?

That is the question we are obliged to ask ourselves, however much we deplore the sacrifice of individual life, however much you and I may personally detest and abjure the use of force.

To pick up another argument from Hyams, surely we never used to make such a fuss about the sanctity of human life? Surely it is only the Romantic movement, now sunk to the level of the mass media, which has made such a fetish of it? This is not to be a fascist, but a classicist: violent death, mass dying for no personal fault has always been part of the human condition. We are all going to die in the end: homicide in war is honoured and justified in every society there has ever been— why should ours be the exception? The oppressor has put himself at war with the oppressed and must take the consequences. As for the oppressed, his choice may be the unpalatable one between death and dishonour, but he is not compelled to choose death. What is any one of us, that we make so much fuss about our own piddling importance, or that of any other of our fellow grains of sand?

Much of this is true if you like that sort of thing. But if you don't, it is totally false. It is debatable that human life has only recently acquired its aura of sanctity: ancient literature is full of laments and protestations at individual deaths, from the Greeks and Hebrews to the Norsemen and the Gaels. What is recent is that the prospect of living to an enjoyable old age without pain or poverty has given the ordinary man something better to look forward to than a short life and a gay one: and that the meaning of war at its worst has been brought home from the battlefield by the poet, the reporter and the cameraman and laid before the soldier's family in every detail but the final horror of its smell.

The seeds of romantic individualism, with its emphasis upon freedom of choice but without its God-less arrogance, have always been there in the Jewish-Christian tradition. From the days of Eden, our kind of Adam has demanded 'Who am I?' and has grappled with the complex answer: 'I am what I choose to choose from what my society and my parents offer me.' If we choose not to choose at all, if we accept without objection what is presented to us, then we are no more than grains of sand. At least we are absolved of higher responsibility. But if we choose to choose, choosing either to fight or not to fight for the interests of our society, then whatever our fate may be it has a very different meaning. From which it will be clear that, for me, the key question that opens the door to the moral philosophy of each one of us is: 'What kind of person do I think I am?'

To be of a kind, though, is to belong to a class. Most of us easily enough reach the conclusion that we belong to the class of the majority of our fellows; and if necessary we go cheerfully off to war with them. We would feel uneasy isolated from them, and still more uneasy to find ourselves opposed to those whom we instinctively recognise as having dominance and leadership over the nation. Even—and one might say especially —those popular democracies which claim to embody the will of the masses search avidly for named and known leaders to follow, and at no time more than in war.

It might seem that the most valuable thing I could do at this point would be to print a list of the known causes of war. But that would be an illusion. The causes of wars are highly particular and enormously complex, and it would be of little practical value in stopping a new war to weave a pattern of theory embracing the old ones. The same conditions of leadership prepared to use force, of disappointed expectations and complaints of injustice usually apply to outbreaks of violence between nations, as between groups. But there must also be an elaborate concatenation of popular states of mind, conceived material interests, military organisation, political forces, and the breakdown of communication by language. As with any other kind of force, war is an attempt not so much to achieve something as to say something—something about the identity and *rightness* of the nation.

It too much belittles the human beings involved to deny that wars are triggered by particular events that seem at the time to matter greatly; that there are real threats of aggression and real conflicts of interest; and that if these had not occurred, war would not have happened. But the question here is: who defines those interests and identifies those threats? Why, for example, should President Johnson have assured his people that unless the Marxist nationalists of North Vietnam were prevented from overthrowing the upper-class military government of South Vietnam, Communism would soon be lowering its landing-ramps on the beaches of California? This could only have been the subjective judgment of the late president and his advisers. There was no measurable evidence for this overriding assertion. What kind of men could have reached such a conclusion, a conclusion that cost more than forty thousand American lives and many times more Vietnamese?

An American reporter who had ploughed through the forty-seven volumes of the so-called Pentagon Papers on the origins and conduct of the Vietnam War once remarked that it was like stepping through the looking-glass into a world of entirely different values and even language. The people in it seemed to be breathing a different atmosphere from that of the ordinary citizen, or even the Congress and judiciary: a secret atmosphere which they believed to be somehow more 'real', more 'true' than that of the world outside.

It is an atmosphere beautifully described in Richard Barnet's work *The Roots of War*[8] which (though it deals again with the American situation) applies with national modifications to almost any sophisticated state. Barnet points out the American illusion, based probably on the nature of the constitution, that a trained lawyer can tackle anything. He argues that the elite club of lawyers, bankers and businessmen who hold most of the top jobs in the White House, the State Department, the Pentagon and the intelligence networks, has become a self-contained society which conceives *its* interests (not just material investments, but intellectual concerns as well) to be the nation's interests. And just as generals are always preparing to fight the last war rather than the coming one, the security management is usually trying to defend interests that no longer are really valid, and to defend them in outmoded ways.

For a start, it does not follow that emerging revolutionary nations will refuse to supply the capitalist west with their traditional raw materials, or that feudal monarchies like Saudi Arabia and the Gulf sheikhdoms can be relied upon to do so, though much western intervention East of Suez has been based upon the assumption that these are so. If America has become dangerously dependent upon foreign sources of supply since the Second World War, and Britain too, there are two remedies that should reasonably be applied: first, to avoid antagonising those sources by hostile interventions, and second to reduce dependence upon them both by finding other sources and by cutting out wasteful consumption. The spread of multi-national companies has, if anything, given American capitalism a vested interest in peace, not war. For war distorts the economy, diverting labour and upsetting supplies and distribution. Pacifism (as Schumpeter wrote as long ago as 1919) is the natural philosophy of capitalism: war only persists because of the survival of mediaeval, pre-capitalist values like militarism, national glory and the holy war.

The communists, unfortunately, cannot afford to agree. They have been insisting for years that capitalism means imperialism and imperialism means war. Free the colonies and capitalism must collapse; destroy capitalism and war will vanish. Lenin seemed to think that war was the result of rivalry between expanding capitalist empires. It can be; but on the other hand the Red Army has only operated, since 1945, against fellow-communists like the Hungarians, the Poles, the Czechs and the Chinese. To abandon long-held communist dogmata in the face of passing facts would be to call in question the identity of a lifetime, however.

Much the same is true of the American security managers. From Dean Acheson to John Foster Dulles and on to Dean Rusk, Walt Rostow, McGeorge Bundy, Robert McNamara and George Ball, they have all adopted a Manichean view of the world balanced between Good and Evil, with the United States driven by its mission to carry forward its banner with that strange device of Freedom. It has something to do, I believe, with the very act of separation and setting apart— semi-religious in origin—which gave birth not only to the United States as a nation but to every new-immigrated American. American Foreign Policy has long been regarded as a superior type of moral philosophy, and the security managers of the United States have all been profoundly moral men.

But of late this has become both embarrassing and hampering. There comes a point beyond which it is impossible to present a Latin American military junta as guardians of freedom, however much American investment they may be sitting on. And so a newer strain of realism, in the jargon 'pragmatism', has crept into the managerial offices, making it all the more necessary to seal them off from the naively idealistic public. Enlightened self-interest is the essence of all the best foreign policy; but enlightenment is one thing, cynicism another. The managers believe, says Barnet, that man has a taste for violence that can only be kept in check by the best among us—the successful who have risen to the top of the professions of power. For they are 'the achievers'. It hardly matters what they have achieved, so long as they show a talent for using power and, above all, are fearless in the use of it. The appeal of power, rather than that of money, is what makes them tick,

Under any of the more elaborate power structures of our time, the job of the security manager is to present his master with simplified options. Complicated doubts and fears are not wanted: the evidence of competence is a tough, lean analysis and a positive plan of action. Fast, fact-loaded nitty gritty, digests of the press (not the papers themselves)—that is the breakfast diet of today's with-it presidents and prime ministers.

Both the American and the Russian cultures seem to encourage toughness, diplomatic virility. The other side, it is argued, only understands force and will regard compromise or concessions as evidence of weakness. From this it follows that an ability to see the other side's point of view—for example, that of the North Vietnamese or the Arabs or the Russians—is a grave handicap in the security manager's record. An unquestioning sense of the national mission, backed by a fierce and impatient sense of loyalty to the team, a readiness to lie for the cause, even to resort to physical dirty-tricks, are the badges of the high-flying security aide.

It is, of course, hard for anyone to abandon old habits, old errors, old clichés of thought; but in the all-male changing-room atmosphere of a White House basement or a policy-planning group the game of self-justification can lead to disaster on a global scale. It is even harder to withdraw an unsuccessful policy for national security than an unsuccessful motor-car like the Edsel. Most dangerous of all, the worship action, results and toughness, combined with the group's remoteness from the world of the public, can lead with little hesitation to mass-murder by bureacracy. There is a convenient division of labour built into modern warfare; as Barnet puts it: 'Those who plan do not kill, and those who kill do not plan.' It has a routine, unemotional efficiency about it, separating killer from victim almost as much as it separates them both from the planner, that helps to reinforce the alienation, the 'otherness' of the enemy upon which all organised violence must be based.

The claim that Vietnam threatened the national security of the continental United States might just, within the generously extended bounds of logic, have been true—in which case it would have been equally important to examine the motives of the North Vietnamese leadership. But in either case or both what is important is the leadership, the leadership *to* war and the leadership *in* war. In short, I do not believe that the people make war: they are hardly equipped to do so, even if they wanted to (which they sometimes do). It is not we the people that make war, it is those who lead us.

And at the level of leadership the effect of blind, deterministic forces becomes remote. What mattered when Poland was invaded in 1939 was less the Balance of Power or Dialectical Materialism than the personalities of Hitler and Stalin and of their inner cabinets. Certainly the two leaders could cite the ideologies of Nazism and Communism to justify what they did, but they themselves were the high priests and in one case the very founder of their religions. It will not do to insist that Hitler was the tool of Ruhr big business or of Prussian militarism. It was they who became the tools of Hitler, becoming so deeply involved that they were obliged to endorse Nazism in order to give a gloss of higher things to the confidence trick.

Hitler's philosophy, fuelled by entirely groundless superstitions about Nordic superiority and Jewish subversion, was a kind of international Darwinism. The fittest survived through conflict—conflict was the father of everything. Virtue reposed in the blood of the race; its might was right; the individual counted for nothing; only the Leader, who embodied the will of the race and asserted it by force, was significant. Race was as central to Hitler (says his biographer Alan Bullock[12]) as class was to Marx. But then Marx was racially dispossessed and Hitler was a social outcast: each, for personal reasons, overemphasised the element in the framework that was left to him.

The leader, though, is never entirely alone. Man has a passion for hierarchy and properly graded status which does link us very clearly with the apes. But because of our capacity for generalised thought in concepts, leadership can be symbolised in flags and isms, and the leader may not be one man at all, but a group, an oligarchy. Even the single tyrant requires a circle of lieutenants whose function becomes that of justifying his ideas and reflecting them approvingly back to him as the findings of the entire governing machine. At their worst, as in Nazi Germany, this circle of lieutenants may come to resemble an old-style Chicago gang which bullies, terrorises and ultimately brutalises an entire nation. The driving force of a gang which has come to power by violence is likely to be the impulse to defy authority. Finding itself in authority, it can only govern by first murdering the law. Much of the writing about violence in the years surrounding the Second World War, like J. B. Bronowski's *Face of Violence*[11], is obsessed with this idea of the permanent saturnalia of brutality, whipped on by a few 'professionals of vice' who eventually make disgrace a national habit. Believing as I do that Nazism would not have happened without Hitler, and that Nazi Germany was an almost unique example of a talented but disgruntled people debauched by a clever maniac, I do not really feel that this is the danger facing us today. However, Hitler's career still carries this lesson which can be picked up by any war leader who chooses to apply it: being a quasi-psychopath, he dared to act where others scrupled, and the action produced results. The secret was boldness.

'A Prince', wrote Machiavelli,[33] 'should therefore have no aim, thought or object of study but war, its organisation and discipline. . . . The chief cause of the loss of states is the contempt of this art. . . . It is unreasonable to expect that a man who is armed will willingly obey one who is not. . . . It is much safer to be feared than loved. . . .' Machiavelli's was the voice of an extremely violent age, though we have come to think of it as one outstanding for the arts of peace. I have only heard of one other in which princes were in greater danger to their lives: elaborate analysis by the American scholar Daniel Tretiak, carried out for the Eisenhower Commission on Violence, reveals that of top-rank Chinese officials in the late Ming Dynasty only 60 per cent died of natural causes, while 13 per cent committed suicide, 13 per cent died in war, 11 per cent were executed and 3 per cent were assassinated. At times like those, when leaders were personally threatened by violence, they had every reason to study the art of self-defence. On the small scale of the average pre-industrial state the theory and practice of war was something the ruler was obliged to master for himself. The army was his army, the land his land, the war his war and its end decisive with his death.

Today it is far more complicated. Nationalism, democracy, even the demagogic techniques of modern totalitarianism manage to spread the involvement in war far wider. All the media of modern communications are employed to persuade the public that the leaders' policies are in fact *their* policies. The people, in fact, have very little opportunity or inclination to work out detailed and reasoned attitudes on questions of national security. And it is all too easy, in countries where civil politics are weak or discredited, to persuade people that even in time of peace the true repository of the national honour is the army and that its use of force is the true expression of the national will. The fact that in many countries the army presents a better cross-section of the nation and is in closer touch with the provinces than the politicians of the metropolis only makes for that most dangerous of all forms of military rule, popular militarism. But however plebeian the slogans, it is the towering hierarchies of the foreign ministries and defence departments, the cabalistic think-tanks of the executive and the self-justifying party machines whose faces and reputations are really at stake. They invented the game, its rules and its language and they alone know what the object is.

CHAPTER FIVE

The Profession of Violence

I INTEND here to conduct a short historical tour of organised warfare and its philosophy; mainly to demonstrate how absorbing it has always been for Man. Throughout this book I tend to write of 'Man', and though there are some occasions where man-and-woman could be substituted, for the most part my choice is deliberate. I do believe that the male must shoulder by far the greater share of the blame for the destructiveness of our race. The difference between the sexes is real both at the mental and physical levels: the male is by nature the dominating, ambitious, aggressive sex, the one inclined and equipped to use force, and the one unhampered (for better or worse) by maternity. It is stupid to pretend that women's liberation frees them to imitate men, rather than liberating them to be truly women and enforcing women's natural interest in non-violence. If the image of Leila Khaled, the girl guerrilla, blazing machine gun in hand, or the Price sisters priming a car bomb for Ireland, appeals to you more than that of Mother Theresa, Florence Nightingale or the Virgin Mary, then it is time to lay down these pages. You and I are wasting our time. Whatever their loyalty to Palestine and Ireland, the Khaleds and Prices are the real traitors to their sex.

There can be no question that war is the occupation of the male, with his urge to demonstrate his toughness, his passion to lead or be led, for group action in the field, and his obsession with tools and weapons. Only recently have women been introduced as drivers and technicians behind the lines. Notwithstanding the exceptional Russian woman sniper or Arab woman hijacker, it remains to most cultures unthinkable that women should be engaged as killers side-by-side with men. For the gentleman, war's elements of art and sport have made it an absorbing hobby and a not-too-taxing profession. For the working man it has provided an escape from poverty, boredom and domestic complications.

Scholars, mainly from among the gentry, have picked out the principles governing the successful waging of warfare with remarkable agreement, for they are largely principles of human mass psychology. From Jomini and Clausewitz[14] in the 1830s, through the Prussian school of the Bismarck era, the British Field Service manuals and on through the mid-twentieth-century writings of de Gaulle, Liddell Hart[29], Montgomery[38], Vagts[55] and Falls[66] the essentials are much the same: Maintenance of the aim (you must decide firmly what you are trying to do and stick to it); surprise and mobility (which recent Middle East wars have heavily underlined); the concentration of superior forces at the decisive point; the effective cooperation of all the arms involved; secrecy; and command control through reliable communications (the department which, with air mobility, was best developed by the Americans in Vietnam—though it did them little good without the rest).

In addition, scholars and generals have their own pet theories about leadership and tactics. Some favour aggressive reconnaissance—though spy satellites and drone photographic planes have rendered that unnecessary. Some worship the elite corps of guards or marines, while others consider them more trouble than they are worth. Some, like Falls and Montgomery, emphasise the need for a commander with charisma who can 'put himself over to his troops'. Others call for a good committee chairman, like Eisenhower, with a talent for selecting staff. Montgomery claims that his battle secret was to unbalance the enemy by forcing him to stretch his reserves over a wide front, and then to apply his main force on the narrowest front possible. Others, for generations, pinned their faith on the infantry manual's doctrine of 'pin down and outflank'. It all becomes as fascinating as the discussion of football tactics, and on this level it is hard to remember that human lives are at stake.

There will even be debate about the purpose of going to war. Victory—but what constitutes victory? It may be no more than the absence of defeat, but there is a sliding scale along which it is possible to pick a definition which goes either too far or not

far enough. Part of the trouble with the Vietnam War was that
the United States felt obliged, for non-military reasons, to select
as its aim the inadequate objective of trying to make the North
Vietnamese leave the South Vietnamese alone. If it had been
able to choose the classic objective, the destruction of the enemy's forces on their own territory if necessary, the affair would
have been over a great deal sooner. At the opposite extreme,
military writers from Fuller and Liddell Hart to Hanson
Baldwin have condemned the Second World War concept of
unconditional surrender as barbarous and self-destructive. The
crushing of the opposing nation does enable one to dictate
terms of peace, but a dictated peace (as Raymond Aron observes)[6] is not always preferable to a negotiated settlement.
Even beyond the extra cost and casualties to one's own side,
the complete destruction of the other poses the questions of
what is to take its place and who is to pay for the reconstruc-
tion? Has not the West already good cause to regret the dis-
memberment of Germany after unconditional surrender?

When wars were properly declared (a process which included the formal proclamation of war aims) it was a relatively
simple matter to end them, either by achieving or conceding
the aims or by offering at least to compromise over them. Total
war leaves no reason why an opponent should do anything but
fight on to the bitterest of ends.

Total war was being waged long before aerial bombing or
nuclear weapons; the history of warfare consists of a series of
advances towards it and withdrawals from it in horror. Even
the Athenians were capable of war without mercy. So were the
Israelites. The Thirty Years War, the most cynical of European
conflicts, may have cost as many as seven million lives and
reached its climax at the sack of Magdeburg and the indiscriminate slaughter of thirty thousand men, women and
children.

Wolves howled through the streets of Magdeburg. To
scholars it seemed the final degradation of western culture, and
it drove the Dutch lawyer Grotius to draw up his code for the
conduct of just but restricted warfare. Basing himself upon the
principles of natural law, since the warring of the churches had
discredited the authority of Scripture, he insisted that war
should only be lawful if grievances had first been stated for-

mally and negotiation had subsequently failed. Fighting should be conducted under rules which respected neutrality, spared women and children, and guaranteed humane treatment for prisoners and wounded. Any peace treaty was *ultra vires* which sought to legitimise the conquest and absorption of one sovereign state by another.

Europe was more than ready for Grotius's ideas. Its vast armies were exhausted, and the savagery of the religious wars tapered off into the relatively harmless marchings and countermarchings of the late seventeenth and early eighteenth centuries. King Louis XIII had issued standing orders to his fortress commanders forbidding them to surrender under siege until a wide breach had been made in their walls and several assaults had been repulsed from it. Louis XIV gently reduced the requirements to one small breach and a single assault[14]. Casualties were light on the whole, and warfare became the art of surrendering gracefully; until the rude shock of the French Revolution, when a fortress commander was guillotined for surrendering to the Prussians under Louis XIV's regulations. The age of modern total war had begun.

Grotius was reverting to the spirit of christian chivalry. I shall be dealing later with the pacifism of the early church: my immediate point is that by the tenth and eleventh centuries the French church in particular, while exploiting warfare for its own purposes from time to time, had managed to contain it within limits which protected civilian society. The Councils of Charroux, Le Puy and Poitiers (A.D. 989–1000) sought to protect the clergy and the poor from the ravages of war and insisted that great lords must refrain from settling their disputes in the field instead of in the courts. At a further Council in 1016, the nobility of France undertook not to impress clerics and peasants into their armies and not to commandeer their crops and beasts. Within a few years a militant peace movement broke out, with unruly mobs of priests and peasants assaulting the castles of barons who would not subscribe. It had to be suppressed, inevitably by force.

But the Middle Ages did manage to establish some more practical restraints upon warfare[60], of which the Peace of God (which protected the property of the clergy and the poor) and the Truce of God (which limited the days upon which fighting might take place) were the most significant. Their application varied between provinces and principalities, but in various times and places warfare was limited to as little as three months in the year and military service to as little as forty days, and no battle was permitted between Wednesday evening and Monday morning. Fighting on major feast days and weekends was widely banned, although it has to be admitted that William the Conqueror did not hesitate to fight the Battle of Hastings on a Saturday, while the Crusaders often excused themselves that killing on holy days was legitimate if the victims were infidels. In 1139 the crossbow was outlawed as too atrocious a weapon for one christian to use against another—though it was, of course, legitimate to fire it against the unbelieving Turk (the communist or Viet Cong of those days).

Alas, with the splitting and failing of the Church, men are no longer even partially united under the Cross. But as long as men of Science saw themselves serving God in a wider civilisation, and not merely pursuing knowledge for its own sake, they too observed certain limits. Even Archimedes, in the third century, thought it beneath him to reveal the secrets of the war machines he devised for use against the Romans at Syracuse. Roger Bacon recorded a formula for gunpowder in 1260, but wrote in code to prevent it falling into evil hands. Leonardo's notebooks are full of deadly military inventions, among them a tank and a submarine, but he held them back, arguing (of the submarine): 'This I do not disclose, because of the evil nature of men who would practice murder upon the bed of the sea.'

Still more intriguing were the devices of the Scottish laird and mathematician John Napier (1550–1617). He was active in the 1590s devising what he called 'Secret Inventions for withstanding the enemies of God's truth and religion'. Among them were yet another submarine, a tank which discharged 'harquebush through smalle hoalles' and a burning-glass to set fire to enemy ships, just as Archimedes is said to have done at Syracuse. Indeed, recent experiments by the Greek Navy have shown that it would have been perfectly possible for him to set fire to a wooden ship, more than a hundred yards away, within a few seconds. Weirdest of all Napier's inventions was a weapon which he describes as a 'piece of artillery which passeth not lineally through the enemy but, ranging abroad within the whole appointed place and not departing forth till it hath executed his whole strength'.

It sounds to me like some kind of rocket-propelled scythe chariot. According to a contemporary Scot, Sir Thomas Urquhart, Napier actually demonstrated this demonic device 'upon a large plain in Scotland to the destruction of a great many herds of cattle and flocks of sheep'. Urquhart insists that thanks to 'some secret springs, inward resorts and other implements' the weapon could clear a field four miles in circumference of every living thing more than one foot in height. But Napier left no blue-print for the armourers. When, on his deathbed, his relatives pressed him for his secrets, he is said to have replied that there were enough devices already for the ruin of sinful man, and he did not propose to add to them. The later inventors of the machine-gun, Napalm and the Atom Bomb, even supposing they were equally disillusioned about their fellow men, did not take so lofty a view of their personal responsibilities.

Man's genius for invention must take a lot of the blame for the fact that war has always been a growth industry. So long as it was a matter of battering away, face to face, with clubs and hatchets, conflict was unlikely to last long or be very deadly. To this day, as we have noted, battles among primitive tribes consist of more insults than blows and are quickly over with no more than a handful of casualties. We know that this kind of balance of fear was upset by the invention first of the bronze, then of the iron and steel sword. But it was a balance quickly enough restored, so that the escalation of warfare was very gradual over the centuries. The arrival on the battlefield of the bow and arrow made a radical difference, for it meant that warfare was no longer restricted to the heavyweights of the community. As David demonstrated with his sling, human technology had the effect of enabling the weak to overcome the strong. The survival of the fittest no longer meant the triumph of the most muscular. Indeed, it seldom has: it has always meant the survival of those who are cleverest at adapting themselves to changing circumstances, which is what Nietzsche was complaining about.

The answer to the steel sword and, to some extent, the bow was body armour. Its disadvantages in weight and limitation of movement could be offset by using an earlier accessory, the horse. A development of this combination was the mediaeval heavy-armoured knight, the symbol of war as the pursuit of the feudal land-holder—specialised, snobbish, as expensive to maintain as a racing motor-car, subject to fascinating rules, refinements and technical developments and far above the common peasant who was strictly forbidden to own knightly weapons. Feudal lords were not, in any case, too keen on involving the peasantry in their wars: it took them away from cultivating the land, and once they had arms in their hands there was no knowing whom they might turn them against. They were not even very efficient soldiers.

The knights dealt effectively with the shield walls of the raiding Norsemen and dominated the small-scale land-grabbing wars of Europe for four hundred years. Like the dinosaurs they eventually became too heavy, too demanding of scarce resources and, worst of all, they were easily dealt with by the common musketeer when he arrived. The gentlemen condottieri of Italy resented this bitterly. At least one of them used to cut off the hands and put out the eyes of any German musketeer that he caught, for daring to shoot at his social superiors.

Gunpowder was known in Europe as early as the thirteenth century. It was probably introduced from the Orient as blasting powder in the mines. We hear of cannon early in the fourteenth century, but they had no serious effect upon battles until the middle of the fifteenth. The really significant development was that of mobile guns, accurate hand-weapons and of better shot and powder about fifty years later. In 1503 the battle of Cerignola became the first to be won by small-arms fire. In 1515 French field artillery was decisive against the Swiss pikemen at Marignano. And in 1519 portable firearms enabled Cortes' tiny force to conquer Mexico.

Horses, too, were vital to his expedition. Here I should reach far back in time to underline the revolutionary impact that cavalry must have had from their first appearance in Europe out of central Asia, introducing an excitement and mobility into battle which made possible the swarming invasions that ravaged the continent for centuries.

Cavalry were not native to the armies of Greece and Rome, where the early tradition was that of an egalitarian militia of free citizens standing shoulder to shoulder and hacking away with much courage if little imagination, convinced that nothing was more sweet and honourable than to die for the fatherland.

There were contemporary peoples far more subtle in warfare than the Greeks and Romans, and better horsed too. The armies of ancient Egypt were carefully divided into specialised units; great masses of chariots could be manoeuvred like tank columns today, and maintained in the field with fodder and spare parts. The Assyrians, the Prussians of the ancient world as Montgomery calls them, terrorised the Middle East for more than five hundred years, thanks to a social order wholly focussed upon war and an army which included cavalry, heavy chariots and mounted bowmen as well as infantry. The impact of this sort of massed force, employed also by the Persians, was almost fatal to the Greeks, whose armies in turn were compelled to become a great deal more mobile and specialised. The Macedonians under Alexander emerged successfully with a combination of the old unshakable phalanx *plus* dashing cavalry, the two elements directed with far more flexibility and imagination than the Asians could muster.

The Romans, too, had been weak in cavalry and strong in man-to-man courage. Being a more expansionist and aggressive people than the Greeks, besides having to counter the Carthaginians, the Romans learnt to put their legions together on a more systematic basis for longer service further away from home. Their passion for digging fortified camps has left its mark all over western Europe. But this expansion meant the hiring of barbarian forces, especially light units and cavalry, and the induction into the legions of unemployed Roman riff-raff looking for loot. The free citizens' militia was disarmed and sent home, and the dangers of a standing army full of barbarians and commanded by a professional military dictator became all too clear. Emperors tried to protect their personal positions by raising a Praetorian Guard, the prototype of the coup and counter-coup force of modern times. The Praetorians played their part in the decline and fall of both the western and eastern empires.

And so we arrive at feudal Europe with armies raised once more *ad hoc*, the king summoning his vassals and specifying the number of knights and the supplies and equipment required of them. But this was still a Europe on the defensive against the barbarian, which helps to explain why a christian Europe had not become a pacifist Europe. The defensive nature of the struggle against the Vikings, the Moors and the Turks explains why for so long the castle was the dominant piece on the board, with the heavy knight beside it. Even the crusades turned into a defensive operation: Asia had lessons to teach about mobility and the combination of horse and foot, but they were not properly applied until much later, first in Renaissance Italy, then along the Baltic.

Italy had shown the value of trained professionals using fire-arms. But, as Machiavelli complained, mercenaries tended to be half-hearted and of transferable loyalty. Gustavus Adolphus, the military genius of seventeenth-century Sweden, conscripted his own subjects but paid them properly and equipped them with standardised weapons of advanced design. He broke down his large units into small, easily-handled platoons and sections and saw that they were properly drilled, instructed and sup-plied. Gustavus's tactics were highly scientific. He understood the use of rapid-firing field artillery and combined it flexibly with highly-disciplined cavalry and with musketeers who were protected, while they reloaded, by hedges of pikemen. Crom-well's New Model Army, of the English Civil War, was based on this Swedish model.

The growing strength of central governments during the seventeenth century, and of the economic resources at their command, brought an enormous increase in the size of armies. The Middle Ages would have been impressed by a force of fifteen thousand men: Louis XIV put more than ten times that number in the field, and Frederick the Great raised in tiny Prussia an army of two hundred thousand. Swiss, Swedish, German and Scottish mercenaries continued to hire themselves out (one of my mother's ancestors fought Napoleon for the Czar, and was known as 'the Russian Renny') but national armies, which were normally the kings' armies, were ex-clusively officered by landed gentlemen who were expected to subsidise their units from their own pockets, just as the feudal knights had done. Standing armies were never popular, but it was rare to find a country like England which, having subdued its monarchy and to enfranchise the middle classes, could remove the army from autocratic control.

As firearms improved and the use of the bayonet spread, the clumsy pikeman dropped out and battles became still more mobile. The British under Marlborough began their emphasis upon marksmanship and controlled volleying, followed in the last resort by cold steel, which remained their strongest point for some two hundred years. For the greater part of that time it was effectively combined with the ability to hold off cavalry charges by forming squares.

But the mid-eighteenth century saw the ominous influence of the two Fredericks, father and grandfather of Prussian militarism, for all their other gifts. Frederick William I was the initiator of what we consider Prussian discipline—the constant drill and ruthless punishment that made men fear their officers more than the enemy and go forward sooner than run back. Behind this, he and his son Frederick the Great built up a civil service, a military staff and a war college that were able to direct the talents and resources of the state into a war effort. Honour and glory, however, were still for the gentry. The landed junkers were guaranteed the officer corps, and the militarist state helped to keep the peasantry in its place and to suppress unwanted democratic influences.

Frederick the Great added to this his personal flair for manoeuvre. Under French influence, eighteenth-century Europe had become obsessed once more with fortresses and siege warfare; but like Gustavus Adolphus and other great generals before him, Frederick grasped the central importance of mobility. Confronted with fortifications, he marched round them. In set battles, instead of spreading out in classic line formation, he formed into columns which bulldozed the enemy lines from the flank. But many of the Prussian troops were mercenaries, and as the American Independence War showed, drill and discipline were no substitutes for enthusiasm and initiative. The Prussian tradition was to live on in Europe for years, but in the wars of the French Revolution it was to be eclipsed by new and even stronger influences, those of nationalism, mass conscription and the industrialisation of war.

One thing that had helped to moderate warfare during the earlier part of the eighteenth century was the inability of most

European economies to sustain armies for long[41]. There were shortages of wood and charcoal, of iron, armour steel and cannon metal, even of heavy draught-horses. All over Europe, saltpetre men were on the prowl with warrants authorising them to search out likely sources of the most scarce component of gunpowder. And as we have seen, men of science were reluctant to encourage the arms race of the times by allowing their talents to be exploited. What was the good, asked Samuel Johnson (prophetically), in letting evil men learn how to fly?

In any case, the Age of Reason was so convinced that war was contrary to the rational interests of man, it took it for granted that its end must be in sight. Very similar arguments were heard more than a century later, as the First World War approached.

On the contrary, from the middle of the eighteenth century, the conditions for modern warfare were beginning to take shape. Populations multiplied; road networks became efficient for the first time since the Romans; and the early industrial revolution began to provide coal, iron and all the necessary raw materials. Overseas colonies provided timber, cordage, saltpetre, if not yet very much in the way of fighting manpower. Life and materials were now available to spare—and to waste. For the next century and a half, from the French Revolution through two Great Wars, generals were able to slog it out with an extravagance undreamed of by their predecessors. No less astonishing was the ability of industrialised Europe to recover from their extravagance and replace the losses.

The French Revolution and its wars grew out of a vast collision of forces—intellectual tumult, social, political and economic frustrations, territorial greed and personal animosities, all exploding together. It was at the same time the last of the peasant revolts and the first of the urban class wars. The collapse of Christendom was complete, and the churches were now fatally exposed within each state as having become the chaplains of a heartless social order. With church and king toppled, a dangerously romantic concept of the Nation, the Republic as the supreme unit took over. And there was no more positive way of identifying the Republic and its citizens than finding enemies and fighting them.

The army was discredited along with the class it had served.

Frenchmen heard with fascination of the citizen armies of the American Revolution which had dispensed with mercenaries, fancy drills, uniforms and supply trains and (at times) with the accepted codes of warfare between gentlemen. Two states, Massachusetts and Virginia, had introduced conscription. Above all, the revolting colonies had been fired with popular national ideals, not with territorial ambitions on behalf of the reigning family.

The administrative confusion of France during the early years of the Revolution led to a totally new kind of army, one in which the glory of war was no longer reserved to a warrior class but in which the humble citizen could now identify himself. Unfortunately, now that it was no longer the army of King Louis but of the French people, its commitment against the enemy was bound to be more hysterical and its impact more catastrophic. Gradually order was reasserted, however, and in 1798 the first European mass conscription laws were passed, requiring the registration and call-up by classes first of men between the ages of twenty and twenty-five, eventually of all able-bodied Frenchmen. And with the conscripts came the political commissars to maintain the revolutionary fervour. Chair-borne ministers far from the scene of butchery now had the ability to gamble thousands of lives where casualties had once been counted only in hundreds. The Revolution sent a million Frenchmen to their deaths and perhaps three or four times as many foreign troops[55]. It was the birth of what Barnet[8] calls 'bureaucratic homicide—those who plan do not kill, and those who kill do not plan'.

But Napoleon did both. He brought to the armies of the Revolution his undoubted skills in the field, his grasp of intelligence, thorough planning, the recognising of talent wherever it lay and the exploitation of his personal charisma to boost the morale of his men. In action, he had Montgomery's secret of concentrating force where it mattered. By cutting down on baggage trains and having his men live off the land like the Americans, Napoleon increased their mobility, though at the same time he ensured their unpopularity with the civilians off whose land they were living. In many ways, as Vagts puts it, Napoleon was a military counter-revolutionary. He promoted officers of humble origins on their merits, but promptly loaded them with titles. By modern standards he became grossly extravagant in his expenditure of men, convinced always that his own vision of the outcome was worth any number of common lives, and increasingly spendthrift of the only resources he could rely on, the manpower and revolutionary devotion of the French people. Had he been anyone else he would surely have been courtmartialled for the 1812 campaign: of the 450,000 men who entered Russia, barely 30,000 came back. The luckiest of his corps lost 63,000 men out of 66,000, the huge majority of them not to enemy action but to disease, exhaustion, exposure and starvation.

And yet there were intelligent men, men of power, who far from being revolted by Napoleon's titanic squandering of life were enthralled by it. To some German military thinkers, their appetites already whetted by the two Fredericks, it was a revelation, something they wished they had thought of first. Gneisenau appreciated that if ever a German popular army was to fight for its homeland with Napoleonic fervour, the people would have to receive certain liberties at last and feel grateful to their government for them. If they were to be conscripted without resentment, they could no longer be treated as serfs. This greatly perturbed the Prussian gentry, as did the contention of Scharnhorst that officers should be created on merit. But between 1807 and 1814 reforms were put in hand, though the hand was a paternal one. The last vestiges of feudalism were abolished by royal decree and universal conscription was introduced. At first it seemed a cunning way of circumventing the limitations imposed by the French upon the size of the Prussian army: a small cadre of professional officers and instructors was maintained and conscripts passed through their hands for intensive training, a period with the colours, and then on into the reserves. It only remained to organise and rehearse a system of rapid mobilisation, much facilitated by the arrival of the railways, and Prussia became the dominant European land power from the mid-nineteenth century to the mid-twentieth. It took her seven weeks to defeat Austria in 1866 and four weeks to beat France in 1870. She very nearly repeated her success in 1914, and in 1939–41 she achieved most of what Napoleon had achieved, in very much less time and with fewer casualties.

But instead of liberty, equality and fraternity the Prussian armies were to be inspired by the newborn German nationalism and by a terrible romantic reaction away from the Age of Reason—an Age which, for all its fallacies, had tried to find a rational substitute for the brotherhood of Man under God. Throughout the Napoleonic wars, the British army had remained organised along surprisingly feudal lines. The landed aristocracy which continued to lead it shied away from the risk of revolution that a conscript force with officers appointed on merit would have involved. The British for their part continued to regard war as a sort of game which the British were bound to win principally because they were not foreigners. But in Germany it was more methodical, a mixture of art and science with religious overtones; an ordeal instituted by God to weigh nations in the balance and reject those found wanting. Clausewitz, who had served both Prussia and Russia against Napoleon, preached the most drastic of doctrines[14].

War, he taught, was an act of violence pressed to the uttermost. The object was to disarm the opponent and oblige him to obey one's will. Since victory must go to whomever used the greater violence, it followed that moderation was inexcusable and that force must be applied unsparingly and without regard to the bloodshed involved. War (wrote Clausewitz) was a wonderful trinity composed of the original violence of blind hatred, the interplay of probabilities and chance, and the rational exercise of political skill. It was not so much an art or a science as a province of social life: most of all it was like competition in business, or (he wrote elsewhere) like gambling.

Germany took Clausewitz to heart, something the French did not realise until far too late. And yet, although the philosophy of violence (as applied by Bismarck) succeeded in 1870, it led to Germany's own downfall in two successive World Wars. After the First, the German general staff persisted with the myth that the army had never been defeated—that it had been stabbed in the back by the civilians. But the fact was, the insistence on pushing violence to its utmost bounds—invading neutral countries, attacking civilian targets, sinking merchant ships without warning—could only provoke the other side into doing the same and rule out all the possibilities of statesmanship. As Liddell Hart observes,[29] the doctrine of total frightfulness led to Germany's complete exhaustion in 1918 and 1945. It also obliged her to take the role of aggressor, for only the aggressor can hope to win a war on these terms.

There were two more important stepping-stones between the Napoleonic and the First World War: the Franco-Prussian War and the American Civil War. The former proved Germany's mastery of mobilisation and mobility; the second was really the first modern industrialised war, won as much by technology and economics as by bloodshed. Both were used as testing grounds for many of the artillery and small arms pieces that were to take so many lives in the new century ahead. Even so, armies continued to cling (as they always have) to the weapons of the past, to the horse, the sword, the bayonet and the non-automatic rifle. The British might have introduced the machine-gun in the 1880s, but felt it would undermine the celebrated marksmanship of the individual soldier. Time after time, and not only in Britain, civilian politicians have saved the generals from their own follies. But between the penny-pinching anti-militarism of the British middle classes and the know-nothing arrogance of the generals, it is a wonder we held the Empire as long as we did.

Logically enough the arm which best served the expansion and nationalism of the British was the navy, a force which, while deadly enough when it comes to battle, never seems able to express the hand-to-hand mass violence implicit in true militarism. The British did not even have conscription until January 1916, a year and a half after the First World War began. On the European continent, however, armies like nations, industry, populations and revenues had grown steadily bigger and bigger. The Franco-Prussian War had seemed to confirm that God was on the side not just of the big battalions but of the swift and well-equipped battalions. The arms race that had followed is sometimes cited as one of the *causes* of the Great War; but I believe it is more correct to say that it was one of the symptoms of the international breakdown in communications. From the time of Napoleon onwards, Europe has seen a series of civil wars within the old European community. Toynbee[54] takes it even further back, maintaining that since the Armada campaign of 1588, there have been four distinct major wars of resistance against the establishment of a united

Europe. In each case a single power or tyrant has tried to achieve such an order of nations on his own terms, and has been rejected in the name of freedom by the rest.

Most of Europe now accepts that, at the economic level if no further, union is for the best. But until the appearance of the American and Japanese trading giants even that was not granted. Moreover, very few people—even among statesmen—can bring themselves to cut the mooring ropes of a national identity. Negotiation becomes a matter of scoring points for one's side; suspicions of bad faith creep in; alliances are formed that create currents of power running counter to what is in fact reasonable. And the more objective and reasonable a statesman becomes, the more he serves wider rather than narrower loyalties, the more liable he is to be disowned by those he is supposed to represent. There is no better way (as politicians have long known) to get a rousing cheer from one's constituents than to insist that theirs is the only correct view of the world, and no better way of discrediting an opponent than to accuse him of accepting a foreign view.

It was in this spirit that the powers faced each other in 1914, with the old Europe splitting at its seams under the pressures of nationalism and economic development, and rivalries further embittered by the imperialist competition overseas. The wars through which Bismarck's German Empire had been forged seemed only to have confirmed everything the militarist philosophers had taught. Treitschke, perhaps the most dangerous of the later generation, urged upon German youth that 'the grandeur of war lies in the utter annihilation of puny man in the great concept of the State. It brings out the full magnificence of the sacrifice of fellow countrymen for one another. In war the chaff is winnowed from the wheat'. The appalling thing is that, toning down the language a little and substituting 'King and Empire' for 'State', many a British officer would have agreed. Our country war memorials still speak of the 'sacrifice' of our forbears, as if they had been offered up in some religious cause.

Europe lurched almost gratefully into the First World War, hoping that it would quickly sort out a situation that had become too complex for political solutions. The participants believed themselves better prepared for fighting than ever before. But what none of them seems to have realised was that while the war colleges had been hammering into them the importance, even moral superiority, of the *offensive*, the weapons in their hands favoured the *defensive*. Trench warfare had begun to develop in the American Civil War and the Crimea; now a well-dug-in machine-gun could make nonsense of the boldest cavalry or infantry charge. Yet both the British and the French believed that only the cold steel of the infantryman's bayonet could really win a battle, and both were prepared to send thousands after thousands of men over the top, convinced that sooner or later—after just one more big push—courage must be rewarded and the Hun would run like the coward he really was. One has only to read the diaries of British officers in Flanders to realise (without ever quite understanding) how they came to take the butchery in their stride, and how the astonishing class structure of England kept the men loyal through thick and thin. I once asked my father, who survived the entire four years of the First World War with nothing worse than a bullet through the upper arm, why he had not revolted against the waste of it all. 'It never occurred to me,' he said. 'We all did these things—human beings get used to anything. If they killed strangers, you passed by. If they killed your pals, you just hated the Germans all the more. That was the way it was.' And that is the way it still is, in any war. It's them or us.

And so to the Second World War, which everyone agreed was going to be over so much more quickly than the First—against the ludicrous Adolf Hitler and his cardboard tanks. There was some apprehension that the Germans might spray the civil population with poison gas and a great deal of time and money was devoted to the issue of gas-masks. But the fact was, its employment in the previous war had shown gas to be a clumsy and indiscriminate weapon, far more trouble than it was worth, rather like the much-heralded Germ Warfare of later years. The tanks, however, were not made of cardboard and the Prussian *panzer* genius Guderian had worked out precisely how to use them in the swift, demoralising shock of the *blitzkrieg*. It was the old Clausewitzian principles in modern dress: violence pushed to the limit, unleashed with surprise, mobility and concentration, and supported by first-rate intelligence, communication and staff work. The refinements made in the tank, the aircraft and the submarine since the First World War meant that mobility and surprise were now available on the widest scale.

The greatest of the new refinements was the aircraft. As a substitute for artillery over the battlefield it was devastating and decisive. But the strategic bomber, with the exception (I suppose) of the two that dropped their Atom Bombs on Japan, seem in retrospect to have been much over-rated. Whether the object really was to wreck the enemy's munitions factories and communications, or, more brutally, to demoralise the civilians working in them, the bombers failed on both counts (as they did over North Vietnam later). Being bombed certainly made the British all the more determined to fight back and not give in: but somehow we failed to make the connection that German civilians would react in the same way. But then the enemy must always be less than human.

The Second World War completed the trend towards Total War. Men *and* women of fighting age were conscripted or directed to war work; the middle-aged turned out as Air Raid Wardens and Home Guards; children were evacuated to the country or the Dominions; food was rationed, land and buildings requisitioned. With the air raids and the threat of invasion, everybody was in the front line. And once again people looked gratefully to heroic figures like Churchill, Montgomery, Mountbatten. Issues were simplified, party politics put in abeyance; when it was all over, a fresh start would be made. The causes of the war had been rooted in the political and economic errors made after 1918. Hitler could and should have been stopped in his tracks and overthrown during his early days, at the occupation of the Rhineland, Austria or the Sudetenland; but given all that, Britain and France could still assure themselves with fairly good consciences that this was a war that the mad, malicious Hitler had been determined to force upon them in spite of their evasions.

This was a far more egalitarian war than its predecessor. With mechanisation and fire-power, smaller units covered wider fronts. None of the democracies was prepared to undergo another Flanders, as the French made clear by surrendering early on. In any case, the pendulum had swung back, favouring the offensive; and the new technologies of warfare demanded education, initiative and skill rather than cannon-fodder. There could be no insistence upon the right social background when pilots, landing-craft and tank commanders were needed by the thousand. Ironically, the atom-bomb was developed to econo- mise in manpower and save life—the thousands of American and British lives that fighting across the Pacific and up the islands of Japan would have meant. And the bomb was so wildly the creature of another century, another world, that there was little shame for the Japanese in surrendering to it. The British and Americans were extremely fortunate that their skills in assembling the bomb had not been shared by the German scientists who worked instead on flying-bombs and ballistic rockets.

Now, the total mobilisation of the Second World War has left the major states with more effective bureaucracies, and in many cases weaker legislative control, than ever before. Much of our social and economic planning is carried out through machinery set up in wartime. Under the stimulus of standing alliances like NATO and SEATO even the passive demo- cracies have more efficient and generally larger defence estab- lishments than they ever had in the 1930s. And thanks to improved statistical and revenue-gathering systems large sums of money can easily be raised to support and expand them. On the communist side, under a smoke-screen of peace-loving hypocrisy, military needs get top priority in the workers' state, and military service for all is unquestioned. It is indeed indis- pensable, less as a deterrent against the war-mongering liberal democracies than as a way of controlling and indoctrinating young people at the most restless stage of their lives. It is almost as surprising that our own disciplinarians do *not* insist upon conscription as it is that the peace-loving Soviets do.

By their dogmatic enforcement of Marxism Russia's leaders are responsible for a rift in Europe potentially as deadly as that between Protestants and Catholics in the seventeenth century. Perhaps it is only their belief in the eventual triumph of com- munism for economic, rather than military, reasons that saves them from being as dangerous as the Nazis were. However, between the great powers there lies the strictly military deter- rent of the rocket-delivered nuclear bomb. The rocket and the bomb are the two major developments from the closing months of the Second World War, and although they are far from being stable deterrents—in that each side is constantly trying to steal a march on the other—they have so far served their purpose in restraining without destroying. The warheads themselves hardly need much more refinement; it is on methods of delivery by land, air or seaborne missile, on counter-missiles and detection systems that fortunes can still be expended. The next Great War could well be one outside the world, fought between rockets, satellites and orbiting destroyers. Already the satellites have revolutionised the collection of hard, factual intelligence, and if the tacit agreement not to interfere with each other's space vehicles continues, the great powers will have learned to clear up a vast area of suspicion about each other's military movements.

Conventional developments have obviously been less drastic: in Korea and Vietnam, the use of the helicopter as a troops transport and gunship; in Vietnam, the use of guerrilla infantry against heavy forces, of light and heavy bombers against ground forces in general, and of a wide range of radio communications; and in the Middle East, the battle of tanks against tanks, aircraft against tanks, and most recently of guided missiles against both tanks and aircraft. It seems to me that with the right selection of portable guided rockets, the infantryman, guerrilla or urban street-fighter could now find himself in a very strong position to take on all comers—by land, air or water—just as the musketeer was in his day. Such missiles are still fairly expensive, but then so are tanks and aircraft, which they destroy. The pendulum has swung back to the defensive.

The domination of warfare by the technologist and the production engineer has meant that weapons are superannuated sooner and sooner. But they are not thrown away or even melted down: they are passed down the line from the first-class power to the second-class power and from the second-class power to the third and fourth. This traffic has been greatly stimulated by the need to combat guerrilla movements, and by the efforts of newly-independent nations to enhance their status with relatively modern armed forces. Dean Rusk once recalled how, while the United Nations General Assembly was voting unanimously for disarmament, seventy of its members were privately petitioning the United States for free grants of arms.

As a result a huge international traffic has grown, with private dealers like Sam Cummings of Interarmco (of Monaco) ready to act as middlemen for the transfer of cast-off weapons, and manufacturing states like America, Russia, Britain, France and Czechoslovakia using official salesmen and demonstrators to push their latest models. The business is worth more than six thousand million dollars a year[51]. Cummings once bought—and sold—six hundred thousand old British ·303 rifles; and the British in their turn sold Peru two naval cruisers which could only put to sea singly, because the Peruvians could only raise one crew; somewhat better than the cruiser sold to Indonesia by the Russians, which was never able to put to sea at all. One has only to recall the cases of the American-made Skybolt missile (which was never actually made at all), the F-111 bomber and the Starfighter (162 of which had crashed under German pilots at the last count) to appreciate that high-pressure salesmanship does not always guarantee a satisfying product. Yet, according to the United States Arms Control Agency, American arms sales tripled over ten years to reach a figure of $3,400,000,000 in 1971 alone.

But it is debatable whether a big arms sale by itself causes war. It takes two to quarrel, and usually (though not always) two rival suppliers to make an arms race. Most people, like the Indians and Pakistanis or the Arabs and Israelis, have other uses to which they would much rather put their money. It is particularly cynical of the Soviet Union to trade non-constructive supplies of arms for the produce of Third World nations. Watched and assisted by their anxious patrons, countries which twenty-five years ago could stage little more than a small-arms skirmish can now stage a battle on the scale of El Alamein, with as many up-to-date refinements as their suppliers dare to test.

What has all this done to the essential nature of war, and to the people involved in it? The public is the last to be consulted about the role it is to play, although the British and Americans have at last been able to return to their anti-militarist traditions of no conscription. In America's case this was largely the result of public disgust with the Vietnam War in particular, and alarm at what the president was able to do, apparently on his own initiative and without restraint from Congress, with a large standing army infinitely expandable with conscripts.

I spent some weeks in Vietnam, at various stages of the war, and found a general insistence among senior officers that it was not Vietnam that had shaken the army with drug-taking, fight-dodging, black-marketeering and a growing number of minor mutinies and assassinations of over-zealous officers: it was the corrupt society back home which produced so many demoralised recruits. By and large, once a unit got into action and men were angered by seeing their buddies killed, they fought as well as Americans in any other war. What those officers did not seem to appreciate was the extent to which the society back home had itself been changed by Vietnam.

Vietnam was undoubtedly the wrong war for the American forces, still heavily conditioned by their engagements in Europe, to get into. It was largely President Kennedy's romantic insistence on going to the defence of 'freedom everywhere' that got America into it. Once there, the mass media could hardly help showing the public just how unworthy and unwinnable it was. If nothing else, Vietnam was the first total-coverage, instant-news war. For better or for worse, that made it far harder for the generals to fight it their way. They tried to protect themselves with a double layer of open public relations in some areas and darkest secrecy in others. The conflict between the two only revealed the notorious Credibility Gap which runs through Washington still.

Meanwhile, the growing sophistication of the weapons devised for Vietnam—ranging from airborne machine-guns that smelled their targets out in the dark to dolphins trained to ram underwater saboteurs with explosive charges—required the call-up of just those youths who were looking forward to their civilian careers. Poor whites and negroes who had dropped out of school early were no longer good enough: the forces needed middle-class youngsters of college standard, and it was that which brought explosion to the campus revolt. Educated Americans could see not only that they had no business in Vietnam, but that the most scientific and expensive form of warfare ever devised simply did not work when they got there.

But Vietnam, like Korea before it, helped to perpetuate in

the Pentagon the military-industrial complex which Dwight Eisenhower, the general who genuinely hated war, had warned against. Such a complex, physically, professionally and philosophically set apart from the rest of Washington, yet with special access to the president, is capable of persuading a weak administration to accept a military view of the world and maintain a military bias to life and business at home. Of all government departments, the war department is always the most business-like. Its managerial challenge attracted, for example, Robert McNamara from Detroit and sent General Westmoreland to Harvard Business School: it has brought war and business into a common world where they can both play the same tough game of self-justification, immune from outside criticism because nobody else speaks their language or shares their inside information (they believe).

Two things, I hope and believe, will keep the military-industrial complex from going mad again. One is the struggle of the American mass media and the Congress to restore the balance of the Constitution away from the Executive and towards the Legislature. The other is economic reality. War, in short, is no longer so good for business, and the world's supplies of fuel and other raw materials are no longer unlimited. A decisive factor in stopping the United States' last bombing campaign over North Vietnam was that the Strategic Air Command was running out of jet fuel.

In the communist world, however, the alliance between the army and the totalitarian party is complete and mutually advantageous. The army is the party army, just as it used to be the czar's. The army keeps the party in power and the party keeps the army in men and money. The state and the army must be one under communism, just as war and peace are all part of the same class conflict. As one Soviet marshal remarked, peace is just the continuation of war by other methods. But since revolution is a politicians' game, party officials have always insisted on directing the army in a political manner.

The triumph of the People's Liberation Army in China has created a new myth about the guerrilla and the People's War. Parts of it are true enough: for many years, the practical teachings of Mao Tse Tung enabled his bands to survive if seldom to conquer. A mixture of terrorism against landlords and sympathy for the oppressed peasants carved out for the communists a series of remote strongholds. They were only saved from annihilation by the Japanese invasion, which enabled the communists to call for a patriotic united front against the foreign invaders. This patriotic dedication won them many more adherents than they would have got without the Japanese. But two things made the eventual communist victory: the growing corruption and incompetence of the Nationalists, and the change-over, after the Japanese surrender, to large-scale conventional offensives using Japanese and American equipment. The Chinese peasantry had every reason to want the old order changed; but the last three years of the civil war were won not by the magic of little red books, but by hard, conventional infantry warfare.

Today, in China, Latin America, Africa and the Arab and Asian world, where people are still trying to escape from ancient humiliations and take some pride in their identities, war may still be naively glorified. Incantations about soldiers fighting for peace and arming for defence (not wholly unknown in the West) ensure that the other side is always branded as standing for aggression. But in the West it is far less easy than it was for our leaders to send millions to death without risking destruction themselves. We are unlikely to hear ever again that War is Good for You. The feeling has lodged that war is no longer fun—that next time it may be them *and* us.

CHAPTER SIX

The Renunciation of Violence

THE MOST acute and compact analysis of public violence that I have encountered while preparing this book is a sixteen-page pamphlet entitled 'Violence and Northern Ireland' by the New Ulster Movement, which has had every chance to learn what it is talking about. It is never obvious, says the pamphlet, whether violence will improve a situation or worsen it. Yet people move towards it as if drawn by some kind of social Gravity, a law of least resistance. Where people are frustrated and uncertain, the easiest way out is to classify some other group as 'the enemy' and prepare to fight it. That makes the situation certain again; everybody knows what to do. And the writer goes on: 'Most of the people caught in and exposed to violence, far from having a clear social and historic conception of its purpose, are swept fearfully along in a malign chain of action and reaction. The vast majority of people caught in this spiral do not understand how things got to this stage and want to get out of it. The paradox is that if violence is the only means presented to people for getting out of a spiral of violence, they will use it—and the spiral takes another downward twist. One of the results of such situations is that people increasingly listen only to their own arguments.'

How are we to break out of this spiral? It is possible to see the life of Christ as a divine pointing of the way: by suffering, by the absorption of violence, by refusing to give the spiral another twist. So we are now in the realm of pacifism, passive resistance, non-violence, non-resistance, the various forms of anti-violence which are related but not identical.

Although through most of human history war has been regarded as a necessary evil—if evil at all—sentiments against violence can be traced back long before Christ. Lao Tzu of the sixth century B.C., Confucius of the fifth and Motse of the fourth all argued at least against aggressive warfare; and the Buddha, as historical a figure as Christ, who lived and preached in north-eastern India up to about 483 B.C., went much further, insisting upon abstention from all violence. Among the precepts of the Eightfold Path is Right Action, which includes abstaining from killing, stealing and sexual misconduct. The Buddha's message was adopted as state policy by the Emperor Ashoka in the third century B.C., and there are those who like to believe that Ashokan India was the golden age of peace which has kept recurring in our dreams ever since. Unfortunately the evidence for this is discouraging. Ashoka turned to non-violence after a war of annexation which had cost more than a hundred thousand lives and thousands of deportations. He had nobody in India left to fight. He seems to have renounced war less in pity and expiation than from a feeling that, having done everything there was to do, the time had come for him to renounce desire and action and take up contemplation. If it was the right thing to do, it was for the wrong reason.

Nor is it easy to accept the contention that Hinduism, of which Buddhism was an offshoot, is naturally non-violent. Gandhi[21] himself once wrote: 'What matters to the leaders of the peace movement is not what the Gita says but what the Bible, which is their spiritual dictionary, says. . . .' India is, and has many reasons for being, an extremely violent country. She has been at war half a dozen times since independence; hardly a week passes without the police opening fire upon some riotous mob; while overcrowding in the cities and land disputes in the country make for a higher murder rate than any country in Europe. India needs non-violence as a tranquilliser, rather than follows it as a natural way of life. The scriptures of Hinduism, particularly the *Mahabharata* epic, are seething with cruelty, bloodshed and war. The *Gita*[9] itself (sometimes cited as the New Testament of Hinduism) is set in battle, and it is war, not non-violence, that triumphs in the end.

The essential point about its hero, Arjuna, is that he is by birth a *Kshatriya*, a warrior, and it is his bounden duty to fight without question. That is implicit in the whole caste system. Yet Arjuna is Everyman, he can feel love as well as ferocity, and on this occasion it is inevitable that he feel for his enemies, since this is a civil war and they are his own kith and kin. Arjuna tells his charioteer (who happens to be the god Krishna): 'I do not want to win, I do not desire land or booty. What good will they be to me if, in order to get them, I must slay the very kinsfolk for whose sake I should desire them?' Plunging further from the code of his caste, Arjuna protests that even to slay the evil can bring nothing but evil in its train. Even if they are determined to slay us, we who know the consequences of violent destruction cannot will to slay them. 'I will not fight!' declares the warrior, and the shock of those words when first the poet uttered them must have been electric: they were blasphemy on the lips of a *Kshatriya*, yet everyone at some time had felt the tug of pity, and here it was doubly justifiable, for Arjuna was being required to violate another fundamental rule of the orthodox Hindu, reverence for family. It was a hideous dilemma.

Krishna's answer would appal many conscientious christians: what must be, must be. And his sermon goes on in the tones of a regimental chaplain: this is the *dharma yuddha*, the just war, and there can be no greater good for a soldier than to fight in it. To forego such a battle as this is to forego honour and duty— it is a sin. Dishonour is far worse than death, to which we must all come. Comfort yourself that weapons cannot harm the spirit. Real peace is only in the mind and can only be attained by forsaking personal desires and attachments, even such noble ones as the desire not to destroy others.

At first Arjuna is not so easily reconciled to his duty. If all that is so, he retorts, why do you urge me to action at all? Man's nature, replies Krishna, compels him to act. We must perform our appointed tasks. We cannot achieve freedom by refraining from action. The important thing is to accept the path of action consecrated for us, free from personal desire. In the service of our fate is perfect freedom. Assuming his godhead, Krishna tells Arjuna that the opposing forces are as good as dead anyway, doomed by him: Arjuna is to be merely the instrument of God's work.

Krishna does, it is true, praise the qualities of non-violence, freedom from anger, compassion and gentleness, as those of the truly saved. But he makes it clear these are the qualities proper

to a Brahmin, the priest-scholar-contemplative, and not of the
Kshatriya, who is a man destined for action. For the *Kshatriya* the
proper qualities are heroic leadership, decisiveness, courage in
battle, devotion to duty. It is useless, says Krishna (bringing the
lesson home to all of us), to try to dodge the battle of life. But
God will free you of sin and fear. 'My doubts are dispersed,'
says Arjuna, 'Thy will be done.'

Thus the *Gita* is the very opposite of a gospel of non-violence
and responsibility for one's own actions. It might almost be
distributed by British Army recruiting offices, along with the
advertisements that read: 'You're non-violent—we respect your
idealism and we genuinely hope the rest of the world will follow
your example. There are still people in the world who will use
force to gain their ends. While this is so, non-violence is likely
to remain an ideal rather than a practical policy.' A statement
which is true enough, though it skirts Arjuna's point which (if
it means anything) means *I* cannot fight—whatever anyone
else may do.

The ancient world had little use for pacifism. The *Lysistrata*
and *Eirene* of Aristophanes demonstrate that the Greeks had
periodic yearnings after peace; but that strange, isolated sect
the Essenes—among whom Christ may have lived—are the
first we know of after the Buddhists who seem to have renounced violence not just as an instrument of public policy but
as a choice open to the individual. The Old Testament tells us,
in the King James and Jerusalem versions: 'Thou shalt not
kill;' or, as the New English Bible more accurately translates:
'You shall not *commit murder*.' But the Lord God of Hosts had
little hesitation in consigning the enemies of Israel to a violent
end, and freely prescribed the death penalty for a variety of
offences listed in Deuteronomy and Exodus including murder,
witchcraft, idolatry, slave-trading, adultery, bestiality and
striking or cursing one's parents. I am aware that I tread upon
dangerous ground here: the scourge of any sort of practical
philosophy is the fanatic who takes the scriptures literally, if
selectively; who refuses to put them in their historical perspective or to distinguish between what was contingent to the
times and what remains of permanent significance. Such people
are liable to insist, for example, that the Bible enjoins us
against blood transfusion, while turning a blind eye to the

equally binding instructions that we fortify our rooftops, refrain from wearing clothes of differing fibres, and defecate in holes in the ground. Equally binding, that is, upon the tribes governed by Moses, for it is only in that time-context that they can reasonably be understood.

The teachings of Christ about peace and violence have also to be read in their proper historical setting. However divine He may have been, His words were delivered to finite human beings for their understanding in a given time, and were recorded by them in the same way. Whatever else He was, Christ was a first-century Jew, not a pre-dynastic Egyptian or a twentieth-century Irishman.

What did He say about violence? We know that He was capable of anger, that He was not immune from its stirrings. All four gospels agree that He used physical action of some kind in driving the money-changers out of the Temple. But in this He claimed to be representing His Father, and there is no statement that He used His scourge to belabour the people, as opposed to the animals they were selling. His personal advice is clear: 'Do not set yourself against the man who wrongs you. If someone slaps you on the right cheek, turn and offer him your left. . . . Love your enemies.' He also taught 'How blest are the peacemakers', and reproved Peter for drawing his sword against the party which came to arrest Him in Gethsemane. And yet He also said: 'You must not think I have come to bring peace to the earth; I have come not to bring peace, but a sword. I have come to set a man against his father. . . .' Elsewhere, we find Him prophesying the abomination of desolation and the noise of battle which is to usher in the Last Days.

The setting in which we must put all this is the constant expectation of many prophetic sects, including the early christians, that the world was drawing to an end. No action they could take could possibly alter that. Christ made it perfectly clear that He was not a military or political leader, that His kingdom was 'not of this world' and that He wanted no crusade of any kind. He and His followers assumed that the gathering wars of the times were part of the coming apocalypse, a holocaust which would be so terrible that, as in the battle of the *Gita*, the family itself would break up and unnatural conflicts of father and son be fought. The reference to Christ bringing a sword must be seen not as a voluntary choice on His part, but as yet another example of His conviction that He was destined to fulfil the prophecies willy-nilly: His mission would help to precipitate the crisis. In the tumult that would follow, His disciples would be obliged to cling to Him rather than to their own families. He had brought the sword, but others would use it.

And yet Christ is nowhere quoted as reproaching the soldiers who dealt with Him or preaching against the profession of arms or the Roman Army and Empire. His rebuke 'All who take the sword die by the sword' is directed at His followers and seems to be an attempt to emphasise that His was not one of the violent guerrilla movements of the day. The legions of angels He refers to next are part of the spiritual battle between Good and Evil.

Christ never turned away the military men who came to see Him. He made a special point of healing the centurion's servant. But then Jesus had renounced both violence *and* political action, for Himself and His followers, without condemning the practitioners of either. So we are left wondering whether He would really have wanted to be regarded as a judge of *any* form of communal action, war included. It was the individual soul that concerned Him. I am not pretending that Christ can be cited as approving or condoning war—any more than we could cite Him as authority for one man one vote, civil rights for blacks, women's liberation, old age pensions, a national health service or many other public institutions which we like to think of as being essentially christian. There is no reason why atheists and Zoroastrians should not support them. I think it would indisputably have broken Christ's heart to wander through a battlefield; and the picture of Him carrying His banner at the head of a real army, urging christian soldiers to redden their swords in the blood of a real foe is the blackest blasphemy. The point is, I believe, Christ was not much concerned with worldly activities as such. He took people as they were, publicans, tax-gatherers, adultresses and soldiers, accepting what life had made them up to that point, and asking only that they accept His spiritual regime. Those who were called to be His disciples willingly gave up their homes and their jobs to follow Him.

Others who admired Him continued in their normal pursuits, and He made no distinction between acceptable and unacceptable occupations for them. In any case, it would have been pointless for Christ to call for a general abstention from military service, since there was no Jewish army which He might have called upon not to fight.

Nevertheless, as the faith spread, there were christian soldiers in the army of Rome. They must have encountered great difficulty in avoiding having to recognise the divinity of the Emperor, something that Rome was insisting upon at that time as a unifying principle in the Empire, and from which only the Jews had exemption—a privilege which no orthodox Jew would allow a heretical christian to share. By refusing to worship the Emperor or the idols, by living in the community yet holding themselves aloof from its company and its pleasures, as if they were only briefly in transit before the Second Coming, christians made themselves unpopular, suspected, and persecuted. The ordeal began under Domitian, and is described allegorically in the Book of the Revelation. Consequently service in the army became rare for christians, and the early fathers of the church found good reason to denounce and forbid it. Christ, they pointed out, had commanded us to love our enemies, and by ordering Peter to return his sword to its scabbard He had symbolically disarmed all his followers. Tertullian, Justin Martyr, Marcion, Origen, Cyprian, all found it to be the christian's duty to refuse military service. By A.D. 180 this refusal had been added to the list of reasons why christians were accused of hating the human race and sabotaging public harmony.

And yet they survived, often respected locally for their steadfastness, honesty and family virtues. From time to time the tide of persecution would recede, only to return with the next emperor, rising to a climax under Diocletian early in the fourth century.

But the faith was not rooted out; and abruptly, with the conversion of Constantine to a religion which was shared by no more than one in ten of his subjects, it soared to supremacy. Christianity came to power at precisely the right moment to heal and consolidate a bruised and battered Empire. Having conquered in the sign of the Cross, the army was clearly now a sacred instrument for the defence of the faith against the pagan barbarians. Military service gradually became acceptable once more, and within a century and a half *pagans* were being excluded from the army and there was a death penalty for denying the doctrine of the Trinity.

Eventually, however, christian soldiers had to explain the fact that, even with the Cross of Jesus going on before, they did not always return victorious. Rome itself fell to the pagans within a century of Constantine's conversion. Assuming the pagan deities were false, how could this be? Was it God's will that the Empire should fall as a punishment for its sins? In which case, was it right to fight for the Empire at all? At this point, St Augustine of Hippo stepped in with a christian re-working of Cicero's theory of the Just War. The Bible showed that the unjust might be allowed to triumph for a while and for a purpose, and that purpose might well be their ultimate destruction at the hands of the godly. It was even possible to make war in love, loving the sinner while fighting the sin. For while you might slay your enemy in the body, his immortal soul could never die. War, however, could only be declared by the divinely anointed ruler, and without his orders no subject should ever lift his hand in anger. Being prayerfully convinced that his cause was just, the ruler must wage war under humane and chivalrous conditions and with the sole objective of restoring peace. Priests were in a special position: they must always abstain from violence, since their hands touched God in the Eucharist and must not be defiled with blood.

Touched up later by Aquinas, Augustine's doctrine provided a satisfying moral philosophy of war, and a retort to pacifism, for some fifteen hundred years. Indeed, elements of it, like the notion of legitimate self-defence and the distinctions between just and unjust, aggressor and victim, live on in the Charter of the United Nations.

Through the Middle Ages and on into modern times, the accepted idea of the divinely consecrated ruler whose wars must therefore be approved by God and His Church meant that such pacifism or refusal of military service as there was became identified with religious heresy. The Albigensians, Waldensians, Anabaptists, Socinians and Mennonites were all savagely persecuted for their refusal to render armed service to their rightful lords, and most of them were either wiped out or forced to abandon their belief—if only in self-defence.

This fragile chain leads us on to the seventeenth century and to the Quakers[62]. I will confess here that, while I am not a member of the Society of Friends and find its founder, George Fox, something of a tiresome prig, I have the greatest respect and admiration for the Society as a whole and for its peace work in particular. One cannot really define the Society as a pacifist organisation, however. Fox himself declined a captaincy under the Commonwealth, but many of his followers came from Cromwell's army and it was not until the Restoration that he and other prominent Friends took up (probably unwittingly) the pre-Constantine position of christians and publicly declared: 'We utterly deny all outward wars and strife and fightings with outward weapons, for any end or under any pretense whatsoever; this is our testimony to the whole world. . . .' But, as always with Quakers, it was no more and no less than the personal testimony of those signing the statement. It was not a prescription they attempted to impose upon anyone else. The unregimented individualism of Friends and their dislike of written codes makes it difficult to generalise about their beliefs. However, the London Yearly Meeting's 1964 pamphlet 'Advices and Queries' (which goes back, in origin, to the early eighteenth century) asks Friends to ponder: 'Do you faithfully maintain our witness against all war, and all preparation for it, as inconsistent with the spirit and teaching of Christ? Do you live in the virtue of that life and power that takes away the occasion of all wars? Are you always ready, with God's help, to work for reconciliation between individuals, groups and nations?' But I fancy Friends would resist any attempt to see this as a catechism or creed requiring all members to be pacifists. Most Quakers do believe that war can never be justified and would never fight in one. But there were Friends who felt obliged to take up arms against Nazism; and even among those who today are opposed to violence in principle, there are some who decline the title of pacifist both because they do not wish to appear to be condemning others who would fight, and because they honestly are not sure how they would behave if confronted with aggression.

The Quakers have always been anxious not to take an easy

way out. Unlike some other pacifist churches, they do not set
themselves apart from the rest of the community; on the contrary, members are urged to exercise their responsibilities as
citizens for the government of their town and country, and not
to shirk the effort and time this may demand. Declining to
fight is only half of their reaction to the challenge of violence.
The other half consists of active work for reconciliation, which
they feel obliged to undertake regardless of any charges of
appeasement or collaborating with the 'enemy' which this may
bring upon them. In so doing they are not concerned with
making moral judgments about which side, if any, is right.
Quakers generally believe that war is wrong and that they, as
individuals, cannot take part in it. They emphasise the importance of keeping themselves 'free inwardly of consent' to it,
and—since they are reluctant to set themselves up in judgment over others—tend to adopt an impressively modest
attitude of 'unspoken but known dissent'[27]. Where this takes
them next is again a matter of personal decision. The great
majority will register as Conscientious Objectors to military
service; but whether they will accept official direction to become ambulance drivers, firemen, civil defence workers, farm
or factory hands, or even refuse to pay their taxes towards the
war effort, is a matter for the individual alone.

The musician Donald Swann (to me a friend as well as a
Friend) was asked by the Conscientious Objectors Tribunal at
Reading the classic question of what he would do if a Nazi
tried to rape his sister? His reply was that while he might kick
him in the tripes, he would certainly not go on to kill him and
then destroy his relatives back home. Unless, says Donald, we
learn to live in God's worldwide country and love the entire
human race, the devil will supply us with the love of just our
own country; and in an emergency we shall be tempted to
burn somebody else's kith and kin on the grounds that this will
help to protect our own. Donald Swann, incidentally, joined
the Friends Ambulance Unit in 1941.

The criticisms of this kind of pacifism are formidable, though
seldom on the same plane as the conscientious objection itself.
(I am not here dealing with contingent objections to particular
wars, for these are *ad hoc* political gestures, and I am dealing
with an absolute moral stand against war in general.) Just for

a start, it is obvious that one cannot kick a tank in the tripes, or tell an intercontinental ballistic missile very sternly to go away. No democratic government could pretend that it was representing the desires of its people by unilateral pacifism, and none that I can imagine would claim that was protecting their interests either. It would not appear to offer a very wide choice between surrender and suicide.

There is the related objection that we are all participants in a social contract, and that if everyone tried to opt out of it when the going got rough, everything would break down. I am not sure it is reasonable to apply this Kantian test of morality: there seldom are many true conscientious objectors and I doubt if many would opt out. But the criticism fails on two other grounds, as does the earlier one. First, the Objector is not claiming that everyone should act as he does. He does not presume to judge others, he is only speaking for himself; and whatever society may believe or even be obliged to do, for *him* to kill would be a kind of suicide, it would violate his conscience-dictated image of himself. Second, the Conscientious Objector is convinced that however deplorable the wrongs that may lead to war, the results of war are even worse. The supposed objectives of the Just War, however solemnly proclaimed, can never be guaranteed: they can never be worth *any* price, without limit: and today, more than ever, war is unlimited. For the Objector it is always and absolutely evil. True peace requires the voluntary cooperation of all parties. War always makes persuasion more difficult.

Quakers, who are no innocents in spite of their idealism, are profoundly sceptical of official propaganda on all sides. The 'police action' carried out by 'defence forces' to 'pre-empt aggression' leaves them unimpressed. Professor Henry Cadbury points out that once the first supposedly aggressive blow has been struck, both sides are liable to fight with equal lack of restraint. Yet does a difference of just five minutes, perhaps only five seconds, make one of them the victim and so entitled to destroy the other, the aggressor? What moral justification has the *defender* really got for lowering himself to the same level? What was the point of Christ telling us to turn the other cheek and of His suffering without resistance the ultimate aggression against Himself, if we are not intended to put it into practice at the level which most affects the innocent?

But again the criticism of common-sense: surely the demo-cracies *did* turn the other cheek to Hitler, after the Rhineland, Austria, the Sudetenland—and look what happened! The *blitzkrieg* against Poland! Can we blame the British govern-ment and people for coming to the conclusion that if they went on turning cheeks, Golders Green Crematorium might have been working full time on British Jewry? Isn't it a good deal more rational to fight tyranny than to lie back and (if not enjoy) tolerate it?

Again the reply begins: others must do what they must do—*I* cannot use violence. We certainly know what the military response to tyranny does, because the tombstones are there to count. The total pacifist response has never been tried and perhaps never will be; but again, that is not the point. The point is one of personal integrity, and the hope that an example may have been set.

Quakers and other pacifists are well aware that once war has broken out, their influence upon its conduct will be slight. They are also aware that others suspect them of moral selfish-ness. So they work harder than most of us (or they should do) to trace and eliminate the causes of war and to prevent relations from deteriorating to the point where people believe there is no alternative to violence. The price of peace, as well as of liberty, is eternal vigilance; for there can be no liberty without peace. Realising that violence steps in where communication through language has failed, Friends tend to be passionate advocates of freedom of information and expression. They try hard, as they did during the Vietnam War at the risk of break-ing the law, to reopen communications that may have broken down. War, they believe, is so evil that it cannot possibly be the lesser of two evils; but that does not mean any evil, greater or lesser, should go unchallenged. Wars break out because men of peace do not see and tackle their causes early enough.

And yet, with all respect for the good, kind Quakers, the criticism must be renewed: surely not all wars are due to mutual misunderstanding? If there was any misunderstanding between the democracies and Hitler, it was that we failed to understand how determined he was upon war. And it is no help saying the Treaty of Versailles should have been written

differently—it simply wasn't. All the signatures of the Peace
Pledge Union, all the loving exchanges of the Fellowship of
Reconciliation did not close the concentration camps. Only
the Allied armies did that. And why should things be any
different with present or future tyrannies?

Once again the pacifist's answer must be: *I* cannot fight.
But (he may add) before it is too late, I can work for peace—
and if necessary I can die for it. It may be that what the cause
of peace has lacked up to now, in order to carry true conviction,
is its own noble army of martyrs. The communists have them,
the nationalists have them, the Black Panthers have them, the
IRA and the guerrillas have them, and they all draw strength
from their blood. But where are the brothers of all mankind,
the martyrs of peace, to accept their fate unmerited and unarmed? For just as the strength of violent extremism lies in the
readiness of its adherents to suffer where their opponents hold
back, so it can be the strength of non-violent extremism too.
The Crucifixion, the early christian martyrs and the conversion
of the Roman Empire show that this is no mere holy hope.
Bonhoeffer, who died in a concentration camp, wrote that the
only way to overcome evil was to let it run itself to a standstill,
not to offer it the resistance it was looking for. Only when evil
met no opposition and encountered nothing but patient endurance would its sting be drawn and its match be met.

'We respect your idealism,' repeats the army poster, 'and
we genuinely hope the rest of the world will follow your
example . . . an ideal rather than a practical policy.'

But it is possible to be active as well as non-violent; and in
non-violent action there lies a precarious middle path. Precarious because half the peasant revolts in history claim to have
begun as peaceful demonstrations on behalf of justice, which
would never have stumbled into bloodshed if the other side had
not struck the first blow. The cry of 'Provocation!' is one of
tyranny's oldest excuses; but some forms of non-violent action
are more judicious than others.

Complete non-resistance has the disadvantage of being, at
best, on the defensive. It allows injustice (a term which I prefer
to Bonhoeffer's rather prejudiced 'evil') to take all the initiatives.
At worst it can look very like condoning or even collaborating
with injustice, though non-resisters may claim they are trying

to win over the enemy with love and shame him into mending his ways. *Passive* resistance does at least permit some opposition to injustice, without violence. And non-violent resistance followed by non-violent *action* takes us from the defensive by all means short of force to the offensive by all means short of force. But let us see how these have operated in practice.

Anxious to escape the entanglements and disasters of Europe, there was great interest in theories of the preservation of peace among early nineteenth-century Americans. William Penn had set them an example by founding his state peacefully among the Indians; and following the idealism of the Declaration of Independence and the Constitution, Americans took seriously the plans for universal peace put forward by thinkers like Jeremy Bentham and Immanuel Kant. But long before that a strain of non-resistance had been introduced into America by Anabaptist Mennonites from Europe (where the Mennonite Church, named after Menno Simon, had been founded in the early sixteenth century). In the 1830s and '40s, a New England preacher by the name of Adin Ballou published a doctrine of Christian Non-resistance which became widely read, in time, as far away as Russia, where it influenced Tolstoy, and India where it affected the thinking of Gandhi. To Ballou, Christ's commandment 'resist not evil' was categorical. Nothing justified the killing or injuring of another human being. The true christian could not employ violence, could not take part in a riot or war, and could not serve in the armed forces or even the civil service of a government which allowed war or capital punishment.

A more practical line of thought was developed by David Thoreau, in his somewhat later essay on 'Resistance to Civil Government or Duty of Civil Disobedience', inspired by the Vietnam of the 1840s, the United States' war against Mexico. Thoreau's personal gesture took the modest form of refusing to pay his poll-tax, for which he was jailed overnight until his aunt paid it for him. But what he wrote was a great deal more influential than what he did.

There was, Thoreau maintained, a frequent discrepancy between civil law and moral law. Unjust laws were passed, even by the most high-minded republics. Yet even Christ had acknowledged the necessity of government, and however burning his conscience the protester must not pretend he had a monopoly of moral truth. Thoreau laid down an exceedingly important doctrine, neglect of which is liable to turn a demonstration of protest into just another crime: the true practitioner of civil resistance must show respect for the law even while claiming the moral right to defy it. He may condemn the law as unjust, but must not try to evade the consequences of breaking it nor question society's right to punish him. Thus, while he defies the law, he is not lawless. He refuses to pay his tax, but he goes to prison uncomplaining. Thoreau believed that a man without a vote had a stronger case for civil disobedience than a man enfranchised. He also believed that one should be prepared to put up with accidental injustices against oneself. What one should refuse to tolerate was injustice to others. When the law was thoughtlessly grinding them to pieces, one should interpose oneself as 'a counter friction to stop the machine'.

Unfortunately the American machine was growing too fast for a few individuals like Thoreau to stop it. The Civil War, not civil disobedience, was the nation's way of putting an end to the injustice of slavery and putting other injustices in its place. Thoreau's ideas were to reach their highest development on the other side of the globe, in South Africa and India, in the hands of Gandhi.

It is doubtful if Gandhi could have produced his version of non-violence purely from the *ahimsa* or 'non-harm' of the Hindu *Upanishads* and the *Gita*. He was a remarkable blend of East and West: as a student in London he read Thoreau and Ruskin and Tolstoy, and even before that he had been acquainted with the ideas of the christian New Testament. Gandhi, it has been said[37], added christian *agape*—goodwill towards men—to *ahimsa* and produced what he referred to as *satyagraha* or 'truth force'.

The literature of Gandhian non-violence is wide and fascinatingly practical, almost as if it were the reverse side of Clausewitz and Jomini. It includes not only the Mahatma's own writings but such books as C. M. Case's *Non-violent Coercion* of 1923, Richard Gregg's outstanding *Power of Non-violence* of 1934 and C. J. Cadoux's *Christian Pacifism Re-examined* of 1940. All of them seek to explain why it is that non-violence should work at all—why it should be attractive to people who do not just want to get kicked around but would like to help virtue triumph. They explain that non-violent resistance can serve as a kind of moral ju-jitsu, causing the attacker to lose his moral balance. If the victim of an attack strikes back, or utters cries of anger or fear, the aggressor finds this reassuring: it is entirely what he expected; he and his victim are both in the same state. But if the attack produces nothing but steadfast courage and endurance, even understanding and respect for the assailant and his point of view, he finds himself completely disoriented. Instead of feeling justified in striking a further blow by the victim's retaliation for the first, or by his cringing behaviour as some lower form of life, the attacker finds no justification offered, finds a superior being. Consequently the attacker begins to feel guilty. If there are onlookers, he begins to worry about his image to others. By remaining passive, the victim implies an embarrassing trust in his persecutor. He may even put him to shame by expressions of personal concern for him.

The strength of non-violence must lie in the adherent's capacity to love his enemy, and to absorb violence without retaliating and without unloving expressions of arrogance, contempt or indifference. But the active non-resister is not simply offering himself as a target upon which the assailant can inflict his frustrations. Nor is he attempting to humiliate or crush his opponent. By bearing witness to a vision of love and truth he is endeavouring to convert the opponent and persuade him to negotiate a solution which will leave both sides in a position of respect for themselves and each other.

Gregg argues that the non-violent resister has at least four great advantages: He really has the initiative—he is not surprised by any turn in the situation—his self-control and lack of anger conserve his energy—and he is enormously impressive, because unexpected. But his outward acts must reflect his inward condition. Non-violence is hollow and even dangerous without love. Love is stronger than anger because it preserves life, not destroys it. But one cannot possibly love one's enemy in a state of anxiety, fear, contempt or anger; which is why so few can be called to practise genuine non-violence.

From this follows a series of practical, tactical points for the non-violent activist[37]: On the principle of fighting the sin rather than the sinner, the protestor must decide *in what role* his opponent is being challenged and try to establish a personal relationship with him as a human being. The grievance must be properly defined and researched, the facts checked and organised, and when the case is complete negotiation must be offered first—as it should be all the time. It is important to respect the opponent's freedom, to ascertain his point of view, and be careful not to drive him into a corner from which there is no dignified retreat. If negotiation is rejected, the campaign must then decide whether to pursue parliamentary action, court action, mass media publicity or what. If direct action is decided upon, the protestors must carefully select the personalities and occasion to dramatise their issue, and if there is to be civil disobedience the participants must be carefully trained. Because not all those involved may prove non-violent, a heavy responsibility rests upon the leaders of the campaign. They must decide at what point to break the law and whether violence can be controlled. All the time they must check local reactions to see whether the campaign is counter-productive. The campaign can be stepped up or down, switched from place to place, suspended to allow negotiations. The campaigners themselves must be as disciplined as a crack regiment. They must be honest, cheerful and courteous. They must be careful not to mock or insult their opponent. They must carry nothing that could be described as a weapon, submit quietly to arrest, and be prepared to step forward into the front rank as the leadership is carried off. Honesty and sympathy are their essential virtues.

I have seen such techniques employed in three continents, in India on several occasions, in the United States during the Civil Rights campaigns and in Britain during Ban the Bomb CND demonstrations. It is a remarkable tribute to Gandhi that his teachings and methods should have spread so far; but it has to be said that on none of the occasions I have witnessed has non-violent action alone produced the desired result. Britain's Bomb, for example, was not banned. Tests in the atmosphere were stopped and the means of delivery became increasingly obsolete, but Britain did not unilaterally dismantle her nuclear weapons. In America, although Martin Luther King's demonstrations undoubtedly stirred the consciences of those who were already sympathetic, it was a combination of federal pressure, court actions and economic growth that really improved the lot of the Negroes. Some of the biggest non-violent demonstrations, like the Poor People's campaign and the building of the Resurrection City shanty-town beside the Lincoln Memorial in Washington, were the least effective. For the fact is, where the mass media are relied upon to produce the impact, rather than the event itself, non-violent action gets diminishing returns. As a news story far away, it soon becomes a bore. As a real event on the doorstep, it is a different matter.

Even in India, Gandhian action was only one of several factors which secured national independence. It is too often overlooked that, for almost a hundred years, the British had been working deliberately towards self-government for India. Added to this was the pressure upon Britain of the United States (a fact sadly forgotten by Indians today). Perhaps the biggest factor of all was the sheer exhaustion of the British after the Second World War, which made it impossible for them either to finance the development of India or to hold down its political malcontents. The public reaction to India's independence as I remember it in Britain was not a groan of shame but a sigh of relief. Nobody wanted our troops to have to stay out there firing on riotous mob after riotous mob.

If Gandhi helped to get the British out of India, it was less by truth-force than by sheer nuisance value. As he himself realised, and often regretted, it was extremely difficult for him to ensure that a march, demonstration or boycott did not become the excuse for violent-minded hangers-on to start a riot; and very often they did. I am not trying to impugn the Mahatma's motives or to deny that he often succeeded in leading the masses away from violence. Perhaps the last years of British India would have been much worse without him. They would certainly have been worse if the British had been French or Portuguese. It was no fault of Gandhi's that Independence was born in blood, not peace; but that again demonstrates how very limited was the power of his non-violence.

In later years I saw Gandhian tactics of civil disobedience used frequently by the warrior Sikhs to secure a state of their own in the Punjab. Bearded volunteers would come dancing through the gates of the Golden Temple in Amritsar, shouting the forbidden cry for a Punjabi-speaking state 'Punjabi Subha Zindabad!' They would fling themselves across a penalty line, thoughtfully painted round the temple precincts by the police, and scramble one by one into the Black Marias that ran a shuttle service to the city jail. Not so much as a hand on a shoulder was needed to get them into their cells. The Sikhs conducted their campaign with magnificent discipline, and in the end they got their way. But it took more than ten years of intermittent jail-going, and success, when it came, was due more to power politics in New Delhi than to the inconvenience caused to the traffic in Amritsar.

The saddest failure of non-violence that I ever witnessed was against the Portuguese colonial authorities in Goa. The British had left India in 1947. The French gave up Pondicherry in 1954. But the Portuguese, who had been on the sub-continent longer than any other established state (including, they claimed, the government of united India), saw no reason to abandon the four tiny pockets of land which, they insisted, were not colonies but fully-integrated provinces of Portugal herself. They refused even to discuss the ceding of Goa to New Delhi, and dug themselves in for a siege.

It would have been perfectly simple for the Indian Army to march in and take over, as it had done in the case of Hyderabad. But at that time the Indian government, which meant Pandit Nehru, was fond of lecturing the rest of the world about the crime of military force, and Mr Nehru himself half-believed (as he told me) that 'men of goodwill, going forward with truth in their hearts and the sacred flag of India in their hands will come to no harm and must triumph over mere physical force'. If the British and French had confessed the error of their ways and removed themselves, surely, he argued (with the logic that anything which should be so would be so), the Portuguese would do the same? But the Portuguese showed not the slightest sign of going, and the native Goanese—who had long enjoyed the best of both worlds—remained suspended between resentment against the Indians for disturbing their cosy way of life, and uneasy doubt as to whether union with India might not be inevitable.

On August 15, 1955, a few hundred *satyagrahis*, mostly from extreme left- and right-wing parties anxious to embarrass the government, started to march unarmed across the borders of Goa. At first the government in Delhi had said it could not prevent them from going if they wanted—after all, Goa *was* India. Then the government advised them to leave any demonstrating to the Goanese themselves, and warned the *satyagrahis* that mass marches could easily get out of hand and precipitate violence. Finally the government lost its nerve and began confiscating the buses taking the *satyagrahis* to the border. Many of them struck out across country and floundered through the jungle for days. Typically, groups of forty or fifty men with flags waving and slogans shouting would march up to a four- or six-man police outpost and try to haul down the Portuguese flag. The police would shout, 'Halt or we fire!' Then, if there were no response, a shot would be fired in the air. If that were ignored, another would be fired into the ground in front of the demonstrators. Finally, the ringleader would be shot. As one Portuguese officer explained to me, in a phrase which became a repeated incantation, 'Authority must be respected—orders must be obeyed.'

At some posts the police clearly lost their nerve and fired recklessly into the advancing crowd. In one case, a Portuguese machine-gunner fired an entire belt into a large group advancing up a railway tunnel. The official Portuguese estimate was fifteen Indians killed, and my guess is that at least twice as many bodies were carried away. I saw one group of captured *satyagrahis* squatting in a Goan village temple, fanning the flies off the body of one of their comrades. In spite of nine warning shots (said the Portuguese) they had continued to mob the post and shout their slogans, until the single bullet had been aimed. Now they were calm and exalted. They were men of intelligence as well as courage: students, teachers. lawyers and journalists. They felt they had done what had to be done. They had a moral right to cross the border and march ahead carrying their flags and shouting their slogans—if possible to hold political education rallies in the Goan villages, haul down the flag of Portugal and substitute the rightful flag of India. Their whole purpose was to break Portuguese law, but they felt that if they broke it without physical violence, violence should not be used against them.

The heart of the Portuguese attitude was that stony phrase:

'Authority must be respected—orders must be obeyed.' To the Portuguese, the *satyagrahis*, though unarmed, had crossed the border illegally and were carrying on illegal activities to subvert the state. If they refused to obey legitimate police instructions, they were treated as a riotous assembly and standard riot procedures were then applied. Another official was quick to point out that the Indian police had just been shooting rioters in Bihar, and added: 'What would the Indians do if the Pakistanis were to stage a *satyagraha* in Kashmir? Would they throw flowers at them?'

Returning to India a few days later, I went to the field headquarters of the *satyagrahis* and found their leaders shattered. One of them told me: 'The Portuguese are evidently not the British. I had never realised it would be like this. I can see now the *satyagraha* method depends on the police as much as the demonstrators. Both have to play the game. Perhaps after all it is not valid in international disputes.' But the rank and file demonstrators, still eager to march into Goa, had no such doubts. I could not convince them that unarmed men would still be treated as provocative, and be shot to death.

A sullen silence followed that disaster, and lasted for six years. Then in December 1961, largely, I suspect, to improve the government's image and give the nation's morale a shot in the arm, the Indian Defence Minister turned his back on non-violence and sent the might of his army rolling into Goa with naval, artillery and air support that flattened the Portuguese in twenty-four hours. Had not Gandhi himself written: 'I would rather have India resort to arms in order to defend her honour than that she should in a cowardly manner become or remain a helpless victim to her own dishonour'? Yes, he had written it. But he had not defined Dishonour there; and one may ponder which did India the greater Dishonour: the continued toleration of the Portuguese flag over Goa, or the abandonment of non-violence to launch an old-fashioned aggressive territory-grabbing war.

Gandhi, though, had always insisted he was a practical teacher. Nations must be true to their convictions. He had no use among his *satyagrahis* for volunteers who were not absolutely convinced that violence was wrong. While he believed that non-violence was infinitely superior to violence, and forgiveness

more manly than punishment, he would prefer (he said) violence to cowardice, if that were the only choice. A man who
surrendered his money to a robber out of fear of being beaten
was no true devotee of *ahimsa*; and one who could not protect
himself or his family by facing death non-violently would do
better to use force against his oppressor. And then, with a
shrewd thrust to the heart of the matter, Gandhi observed that
the trouble with Arjuna was that he really did believe in war.
What unnerved him was seeing his kinsfolk, those whom he had
a duty to love, waiting for him to kill. The *Gita* showed the
futility of war, but Krishna had given the only answer possible
for Arjuna. Without complete renunciation of violence, without complete love, complete absence of ill-will, non-violence
was impossible. One cannot pick and choose those towards
whom one is non-violent.

In short, non-violence requires the extremely rare quality
of saintliness. Not many of us have it, and it certainly does not
come to order. In the depths of the Second World War,
Gandhi addressed an open letter to the British and French
people, appealing to them to renounce war and adopt non-
violence. To win the war, he argued, we should have to be even
more ruthless than the Nazis, and that could never be justified.
We should invite Hitler and Mussolini to 'take what you want
of our beautiful island'. We should evacuate it or, if the dic-
tators tried to stop us, face slaughter; though we should always
refuse to surrender our souls or our allegiance.

I once showed Gandhi's letter to a German Jewish friend.
'We tried it,' he remarked. 'It doesn't work.' Indeed, the
Mahatma had given similar advice to the Jews. Gandhi's
mistake, I think, was in trying to make general what could only
have been the response of rare individuals. Usually he recognised that his civil disobedience campaigns could only be waged
by people of extremely pure heart, profound inner strength and
careful training. Martin Luther King's organisation, the
Southern Christian Leadership Conference, emphasised the
same requirements: it was constantly trying to weed out volunteers who had come forward in fear, in anger, or in hope of
salving their own bad consciences. I once attended a training
class in non-violence at Brown's Chapel in Selma, Alabama.
It was full of good advice on what to do when tear-gassed, how

to curl up for a beating, what numbers to call when arrested. 'Don't give the cops any excuse to use violence,' said the Reverend Andrew Young, the instructor. 'And if any of you white people from up North have come down here looking for martyrdom, we'd sooner you went home right now. You don't call it, it'll call you.' That evening, it called James Reeb, a white Unitarian minister from Boston, who dined at a Negro restaurant and was beaten to death with a plank as he came out.

Like James Reeb and like Gandhi, Martin Luther King himself was sought out by martyrdom. His unique blend of magnetism, militancy and non-violence made him irreplaceable. His death left black America leaderless. Dr King was well aware of his chances of assassination. He told me: 'I don't have any apprehension about it. I'm realistic enough to know that I live every day under the threat of death, and that there are enough sick people in the world for me to come to a violent end as other leaders have. If something happens to me, I will go with the faith that unmerited suffering is redemptive. The thing is not how long you live, but how well you live.'

King was the first to acknowledge his debt to Gandhi. 'The New Testament was a great influence in my life from the spiritual point of view,' he told me. 'Gandhi gave me practical christianity in action, the operational technique.' As for violence: 'I can't understand blacks who claim to reject American values, yet are prepared to imitate the worst of those values, violence. Violence creates more problems than it solves. An eye for an eye is a philosophy that will end up leaving us all blind. Someone has to cut the chain, get off the downward spiral.'

It may just be that by getting off the spiral himself, by accepting the ultimate violence to himself, Martin Luther King did help to turn America away from self-destruction. For although his death in Memphis was followed by some of the worst rioting of all, it saw the end of that particular era. The black guerrilla movements have been venomous, but they have done more talking than killing. With as good a cause, if not better, they have reached nowhere near the violence of the IRA.

So what is the future of non-violent action? Gandhi and his heir Vinoba Bhave talked of forming a *shanti dal* or *shanti sena*, a true peace corps to move against violence and war all over the world and even stage non-violent invasions. There was something of this in the original Ban the Bomb movement in the later 1950s. In 1958, Sir Stephen King-Hall (a former naval staff officer and a descendant of admirals) issued his plan entitled 'Defence in the Nuclear Age', arguing that military force had really outlived its usefulness and become counter-productive. The most that was worth having was a token force along the frontier, and if that was overwhelmed by the Russians, the only sensible thing to do was to recognise that one was better off Red than Dead. And yet, not Red: for the entire nation should be organised and trained for non-violent and spiritual resistance. King-Hall dismissed mere sit-down strikes or making life uncomfortable for the enemy: the economic life should be maintained, so should the administrative machine, but citizens must *at all costs* refuse to do, say or write anything contrary to the principles of our way of life. They must not accept any denial of the rights of free speech and association. They must take every opportunity to argue the superiority of democracy over communism. And they must behave with dignity in order to establish moral superiority over the enemy.

The conception is an inspiring one, but its drawbacks are large and practical. Quite apart from requiring a degree of saintliness rare even in the British, it would call for the elaborate training of the entire population, a strictness of discipline hardly encountered in armies, an unheard of toleration towards armed foreigners in one's own home, and not least a complete political unity which does not exist now and would be very unlikely if the invaders were indeed communists. It would be nice to believe that eventually such an army would go away and let us return to our independent liberal democracy. Unfortunately, if it agreed to go at all, the chances are we should be left in the hands of Quislings to a fate which many genuinely consider worse than death, and might actually include it. If the conscientious claim the right *not* to fight, may not the conscience of others compel to take up arms? Gandhi would say so, and other pacifists can hardly deny it. The pacifist can only urge the warrior not to assume that fighting will cost fewer innocent lives than non-violence, or that while

communism may well be wrong, fighting it is therefore necessarily right.

War is a gamble. But then so is non-violent resistance; and
the state must take account of the fact that few of its subjects
are prepared to take the gamble of non-violence.

Christians, says William Robert Miller, may choose non-
violence but they cannot force it upon others; nor can they deny
that they live in a violent world. Einstein, in his letter to Freud,
cried despairingly: 'Man has within him a lust for hatred and
destruction.' And Freud, in his reply, answered wisely that
human affairs were more complicated: action was rarely the
result of a single instinct. 'When summoned to engage in war,
a whole gamut of human motives may respond to this appeal—
high and low motives, some openly avowed, others slurred
over.'

In the same way, it seems to me, we have to tackle the problem of violence with the whole gamut of remedies and counter-
measures to respond to those varying motives. And surely one
response, in the hands of the right people, is the non-violent
response. Gandhi maintained that non-violence was the law
of our species, as violence was that of the brutes. Through
dynamic non-violence, the pitting of one's soul against the
tyrant, 'it is possible for a single individual to defy the whole
might of an unjust empire to save his honour, his religion, his
soul and to lay the foundation for that empire's fall or its
regeneration'.

CHAPTER SEVEN

The Future of Violence

AT THE root of all violence lies Man's ambition, rather than innate cruelty: his will not merely to survive in Schopenhauer's sense, but to assert *his* definition of his own identity, and his impatience to assert it through the language of force when persuasion and argument have failed. I act, therefore I am. Sometimes we misunderstand our mental inheritance and cannot accept what we fear our identities to be, which is why, in Britain, some five thousand people commit suicide every year, mostly suffering from depression. My own experience was of that kind, and I am only too glad now to confess what I learnt on the psychiatrist's couch: how I had hated my parents for sending me away to a school I detested, how I was appalled by the violence of my desire to punish them, how I came to regard myself as totally beyond redemption and, when my parents died in circumstances where I could hold myself to blame, how I believed myself guilty of murdering them and worthy of the supreme punishment. I very seriously contemplated killing myself, probably by driving my car into one of the bridges on the M1 motorway. I certainly had no intention of seeing the New Year of 1974.

In the normal person, though, there is no such thing as a Freudian Death Wish. On the contrary, there is a burning will to live, independent and yet associated with others by love, by mutual esteem and with the security of an acknowledged place in a social order. Men will resist to the point of death sooner than destroy their own concept of themselves—commit spiritual suicide—by allowing someone else to impose a different image and a different order.

We are not really, by our physical nature, a destructive

species. We have not the teeth, claws or bulk to be so. But we are extremely ambitious, highly emotional, and far too clever for our own good. Our ability to produce tools and weapons has enabled us to change our surroundings much faster than we have been able to change ourselves. At a certain slow pace we do change, and we should give ourselves credit for having adapted as well as we have. There is such an Atlantic of difference between an eighteenth-century African village and Harlem in 1970, the wonder is not that the American black ghetto is violent, but that it is habitable at all. Our territorial instincts, too, have adapted generously to the constant toings and froings of strangers through our communities.

And yet, if what I have said is true, that our technical cleverness has outstripped our emotions, the future of violence is bloodier still—for new technical changes are crowding in, some of them reversing others to which we were becoming accustomed. The motor-car, for example, was becoming an effective (if extravagant and bloodthirsty) way for city-dwellers to assert their individuality and let off steam. Anyone who has driven on British, let alone Continental, motorways has witnessed the ritual contests that take place there. But what is to happen if the energy crisis deprives us of our modern war-horses? How will the virile male assert his skill and toughness then?

I have suggested that at present the facts of modern violence compare quite favourably with the past. It is largely the mass media and our own consciences which have made us, very properly, more concerned about violence than most of our ancestors were. War casualty rates are generally much lower than they were in 1914–18 or 1812. Even in Northern Ireland, Europe cannot show a civil war to compare with Spain in the late 1930s. And the law and order observed in the streets of Britain today would make the London of Her Lamented Majesty Queen Victoria look like a drunken riot, which it often was. The future of violence is sinister partly because we can never be sure we have it under control—it can ebb and flow like a tide, which at present is relatively low; partly because there are far too many objects on the horizon which are likely to precipitate violence unless we can manoeuvre round them with more skill than we have shown in the past.

This is not meant to be a work on current world affairs. But it is obvious that the game of relations between states is now being played on a very different board from that we had grown used to. Europe is no longer the only continent that really matters. It is no longer a game played between a coalition headed by England *versus* one headed by Germany or France (whichever is trying to unify the Continent on her terms). It is not even the game of a coalition headed by England's Anglo-Saxon successor, the United States, versus the Soviet Union (just as ambitious to master Europe). For the United States has lost wealth, face and confidence over Vietnam, and in any case is historically more interested in moving eastwards across the Pacific, rather than returning westwards over the Atlantic. With the likelihood of American disengagement from Europe, the Soviet Union may be tempted to make demands which the Europeans—and belatedly the Americans—will feel obliged to resist by force. Meanwhile the Russians themselves are plagued by the restlessness of the Chinese at their backs; and the Chinese by the expansion of the Russians across the Near and Middle East, into India and the Indian Ocean. The two great communist powers are in competition for the souls of the South Asian and African states, and before long are bound to intrude into Latin America, where the United States will feel even more directly threatened than she does in Europe. Because expectations have risen and been fulfilled the more rapidly there, it is the better developed nations like Argentina, Chile Mexico which are explosive.

This pattern of super-powers has suddenly been complicated by the snapping together of the power of the Arab oil-producing nations, cynically in common cause with the Soviet Union. How long the common cause will hold, and how long the Arabs' own unstable unity, I cannot say. From the Algerians to the Arabians and the Iraqis to the Egyptians and Sudanese there run rifts and stresses which have never been bridged for long in the past. It may be of some benefit to the world if we do all look to our own sources of energy and conserve them carefully, instead of the developed nations squandering the resources of those still developing. But in the short run there are terrible dangers that raw material producers will follow the Arabian example, overplay their hands and provoke raw material consumers into hitting out wildly to teach them a lesson. The Suez Canal invasion of 1956 should have taught us all a lesson about teaching lessons. On the other hand, if we all cease to rely on getting our supplies from whatever source produces them most economically (which is the normal pattern of trade), and instead fall back upon self-sufficiency and protectionism, it is the developing countries which will suffer most and become still more turbulent.

Under a state of world economic siege, the Soviet Union and China are probably the nations best fitted to survive, followed by North America, Australia and the European Community. Their survival is partly a function of their self-sufficiency and partly of national discipline. But in the long run that discipline includes the control of population. As we are seeing already, the need to feed and fuel a growing population, or a large one at rising standards, can face governments with almost intolerable compromises in foreign policy, and so further temptation to violence. The last thing developing nations seem able or inclined to do is limit their populations; therefore, if we are all to avoid violent conflict, the rest of us will have to get used to diverting a larger share of the world's food resources to the under-developed.

Points of friction like this should be obvious enough. Yet concessions are frequently resisted with psittacine cries that charity begins at home and if we give an inch to those communist-agitated black savages, they'll want a mile. Anti-racist propaganda is tiresome music to live with (as was white supremacy), but it has its origin in real history, real oppression, real prejudice. I believe that racism, like economic exploitation, is profoundly unchristian and wrong. But it now seems urgent to me that non-christians should realise, for the very survival of themselves and their children, that these friction points must be smoothed out before they burst into flame. Mozambique, Angola, Rhodesia, Namibia and South Africa may—as the publicity pictures suggest—be full of happy African workers and even happier white management, but anyone who believes that they will not shortly blow up and burn us all had better check what century this is on his calendar. Whatever the theoretical rights and wrongs—and I believe that most of the right is on the black side—it is a matter of practical politics that unless there is a steady movement towards the sharing of power in southern Africa, then violence and disaster are bearing down on it like a runaway train.

The Middle East stands before us now as an example of obvious trouble which nobody could or would head off. The Arabs are entirely correct (if hardly disinterested) in stressing the responsibility of the World Community. It seems to me fairly futile to argue the origins of the war of 1973 back to that of 1968 or 1956 or 1948 or to Bevin, Truman, the United Nations, Hitler or the Balfour Declaration, the Roman Empire or Moses. The point is, another round of warfare was clearly on the way unless negotiation was compelled; no negotiation took place, yet nobody wanted to believe there could be war. The Arabs were partly to blame for having used so many empty threats in the past.

And there are plenty of other examples of trouble in the making which we prefer not to take seriously. Partition is almost always dangerous. The partition of India, and within India of Bengal and Kashmir, still has much violence in store for us. So has the partition of Korea, of Vietnam, of Cyprus and some day of Germany. We bleed still from the violence caused by the partition of Palestine and of Ireland.

Then there are the symbolic strongholds like Gibraltar, the Falkland Islands and West Berlin. Are the principles and traditions they stand for really worth the dangers they are bound to bring? Would it not be a great deal wiser to negotiate terms and timetables for resettling such inhabitants as wish to leave, rather than fight or pretend to fight for them and have to beat a humiliating retreat in the end? If we really are the non-aggressive Free World that we claim to be, we are bound to find ourselves playing the defensive black pieces on the chess board. So it is important not to burden ourselves with positions that are indefensible. Yet we persist in leaving the world dotted with mines and trip-wires for our own downfall.

At all levels the most dangerous of political diseases is the disappointment of expectations, the 'J-curve'. It may affect industrialised nations whose standards of living suffer a setback (indicating, perhaps, Britain, Japan and the United States as now being in danger of civil violence), or developing nations

like India, Pakistan, Indonesia and Thailand where growth
never seems to get off the ground long enough to stay airborne.
However, I believe much of the ambition that drives nations,
as well as groups and individuals, forward is not purely economic, but political and ultimately psychological. Liddell Hart
concludes[29]: 'The more I study war, the more I come to feel
that the cause of war is fundamentally psychological rather
than political or economic.' There is a drive to achieve power
for its own sake, to achieve dominance over others as a nation,
as a group and as an individual; and what we have to do is not
to exalt, worship and justify it, but to understand and control
it. For it is blind and ruthless and cannot be allowed to become
what Richard Hooker called 'the last good of all which is
desired altogether for itself'.

Power, though, is not just the control of material resources.
It is not economically necessary for the Soviet Union's own
supplies that she dominate the Middle East, allow oil for
Europe and America to be disrupted and ultimately, perhaps,
provoke the western states into forceful retaliation or extreme
intransigence. It is not economically necessary. But it is more
than likely that the Soviet leadership, supporting itself on
Leninist Marxism, sees Russia as carrying out a historic mission
to dominate lesser societies. Perhaps the greatest disservice that
Marxism has done the world is that, in Russian and Chinese
minds, it has been transformed into a mode of thought which
is almost impenetrable by established traditions of thinking,
and almost incapable of interacting with them. And like any
other ideology or religion, it depends upon development and
exposition by outstanding leaders. Here the world faces another
dangerous corner, for the leaders of the communist world are
now well past their prime and mostly in poor health. They
have become deeply enthralled in their last years in justifying
their life's work. And it is uncertain who their successors will be
or how aggressive a view they will take of their responsibilities
and their security.

It has been argued, most recently by the distinguished
American commentator Cyrus L. Sulzberger[68], that we are now
in an age of mediocre leadership and mediocre ideas; that the
giants are dead or dying—and a good thing, too, for they
either produce crises or are produced by crises. The rulers of

today are for the most part humdrum technocrats, men of man's dimensions, who get things done efficiently enough.

Which is all very well, but for certain snags: the tendency of mediocre men to attempt to prove themselves great by embarking on folly; the lesson of history, that nations are not content with humdrum leaders for long, but fall easy prey to the thrill of active leadership; and the approach of those very crises which are likely to throw up old-fashioned authoritarian giants once more. In Marcuse, Fanon, Guevara, the extreme left can find its gospels of violence. The philosophy of the far right comes from the gut rather than the intellect, and circulates by oral rather than literary methods.

Recently I had an anonymous, carbon-copied typescript through the post. '*WHAT IS A "LIBERAL"?*' it demanded (hastening then to explain that it did not necessarily apply to rank and file supporters of the Liberal Party, but to those with a small l.) It went on as follows:

'*A "liberal" in the modern sense is a person weak in character who cannot face the stresses and strains of natural life that normal people take in their stride, and who seeks to escape from harsh reality by creating a little liberal dream world of his own where stark facts are reduced to tame abstractions. It is a world where all men of all races are equal because inequality bespeaks the tension that the effete "liberal" cannot bear; it is a world of universal "peace" where the complex interplay of natural forces does not exist; it is a world where all men are "free" in the sense that they need not observe the restraints of civilised society; it is a world where race and patriotism must needs be dirty words since the "liberal" is an inferior example of the former and is incapable of feeling the latter.*

'*He may be readily identified from the ideas he purveys such as comprehensive education, the Queer's Charter that seeks to make unnatural vice respectable, the abolition of capital punishment, mass medication through the forcible addition of fluoride to our water, race-mixing through "integration" and so on ad nauseam.*

'*He is forever speaking of his belief in brotherhood, justice, progress, equality and rights but never of hard work, discipline, or the duties with which are rights are earned.*

' *"Liberalism" is the modern manifestation of ethno-masochism. This is a strange disease, so strange in fact that it is difficult for the normal, robust individual to understand its nature or to realise the extent of its corrupting influence.*

'Unfortunately, in Britain today it is endemic, especially in the spheres of government, politics and administration.

'Ethno-masochism is a self-destructive impulse with an erotic basis. It leads the victim to desire the destruction of his own race, the active promotion of miscegenation or race-mixing being a common symptom of the disease. Other symptoms include a burning desire to see one's own race humiliated and degraded and relishing the downfall of co-racialists overseas.

'In a healthy society the victim would be an outcast and the disease would not constitute a significant danger but when it invades the seat of government as it has in Britain it represents a menace to society that cannot be exaggerated.

' "Liberal" ethno-masochism is a killer. It is the senility of great civilisations; it is the social cancer born of complacency, ignorance and corruption; it is the perversion upon which all other perversions feed.

'When it gains ascendancy, as it has in Britain, the tentacles of deviation reach into every home in the land. It is a disease that corrupts every facet of our national life. If we are not to perish it must be rooted out.'

At the foot of the page, some hand had written: *'viz the inescapable parallel with Imperial Rome in decadence. Luxury and huge wealth for the few, plus "sophisticated" vices; bread and circuses to keep the populace quiet. Withdrawal from the Empire, a huge foreign population in Rome & the apathy of materialism in the face of the inevitable disaster—true democracy having been thrown overboard.'*

To anyone who has read one or more of the recent studies of the life and works of Adolf Hitler, that document must bring a sagging of the spirit. It is all there: the paranoid certainties, the poisoned catch-phrases, the self-fulfilling non-logic. 'If there is one divine commandment I could believe in,' cried the Führer, 'it is this: Preserve the species.'[70]

In a moment I shall turn to the question, what can we do to ward off violence? For the moment, however, I am still concerned with its future prospects. Let us suppose (what is far from simple) that the great powers agree convincingly to respect each other's spheres of influence and resolve any disputes through diplomacy alone. That still would not guarantee peace, for if the past ten years have shown us anything about the future of violence, especially in the Third World, it is that the smaller powers are increasingly ready to use it against each other, regardless of what the superpowers may want. Supposed puppets escape from their strings, or use them to make their masters dance. If it wants to stay out of trouble, a great power should never get entangled with a smaller nation whose language, and so thinking, it does not really understand. Vietnamese and still more so Arabic are extremely subtle instruments of the mind, difficult for Anglo-Saxons and Slavs to appreciate. Cutting the other way, there is no indigenous Vietnamese word for 'democracy'. And yet a war was fought for it.

But even if understanding is achieved between nations, the effect may only be to increase frustrations inside individual states. If, for example, it were publicly acknowledged that the West, the Free World, would cease to give any hope or encouragement to dissident groups in the Communist world, would cease to demand freedom of intercourse and migration, and cease to offer asylum and forum to refugees, then there would be nothing left for the dissident but violence and revolt. Still more terrible would be the counter-violence and the torture which increasingly sophisticated forms of resistance are drawing from police authorities all over the world. It is worth noting, if only as a warning, that violent revolution—as distinct from military *coups d'état*—have succeeded very rarely in recent years. In Cuba, perhaps. In Vietnam and Bangla Desh the greater part of the violence employed was imported from outside.

As hopes of external support fade, the chances of internal violence increase. In part this is sheer frustration, the lack of any other outlet, just as violent crime and suicide increase in time of peace only to decline in wartime. But that is nothing like the whole explanation for modern revolt and terror. To recapitulate: there must be a disappointment of expectations; there must be some basis of grievance, some sense of real injustice—though this may be magnified and exploited, and the alternatives muffled, by dissident leadership. There must be an identifiable group which feels alienated from those in power. Their case is strengthened if there are doubts about the legitimacy of the government. The machinery for transmitting grievances and effecting change must be sluggish or defective. And there must be individuals committed to direct action, with the myths and philosophy of violence to support them.

Northern Ireland is a classic example of all this: rising standards of employment, consumption and life in general had been lifting almost everyone in the United Kingdom except the despised Catholic poor of Ulster. The democratic system in the province was cynically gerrymandered and insensitive. The centuries-old grievances of Ireland against England—many of them true, though sterile—provided all the tradition that violent men could ask for. There was a terrifyingly high proportion of psychopaths and imitation psychopaths among the Provisional IRA: these were men who, from childhood, had been accustomed to everyday, drunken slum violence, and the enmity of authority. And there was an easily identified foe against whom they could establish their manhood and their pride. This was Bronowski's gang recruited 'from men no more flawed than their neighbours . . . but you rule it by a few professionals of vice, so that disgrace is made a habit. . . .'[11]

In what looks like becoming a period of economic discontent and rigid government control round the world, many more pockets of violent disaffection are likely to develop. Times of trouble always lead to inflexible concentrations of power, and this in turn leads to the alienation of small, activist groups, be they miners, students, Welsh nationalists, coloured immigrants or refugees. The only way to pull such groups together with the majority of the nation is to unite them all against some common, foreign enemy, substituting one target of violence for another.

I have no sympathy with the view that Britain's Afro-Asian minorities are a racial poison which should be expelled as soon as possible. I believe, on the contrary, that quite apart from their right to be judged as individuals, coloured immigrants are of enormous value to us as a bridge with the non-white world, with which we had better learn to live peacefully. If we do not quickly recognise that our interest, as well as our moral duty, lies in granting them a dignified identity, I should expect the younger generation of Asians and Africans in Britain to start experimenting with urban guerrilla warfare. If they do, just as in Northern Ireland, the spiral will grind lower and lower. The British Army will find itself increasingly engaged in Low Intensity security operations, and that will be the cue for outside sources to start supplying arms and training to what will inevitably be called the Freedom Fighters. I am not suggesting that street warfare lies in the immediate future for Britain. So far the leadership for it is unimpressive and the philosophy primitive: but the material is there.

As terrorism becomes more outrageous, counter-terror mounts as well. In its 1973 report, Amnesty International warned us all that torture, far from being out-of-date, was now widespread among the most up-to-date nations. Indeed, there is something approaching a public demand for it, bred partly from fear and a misplaced belief in the effectiveness of violent punishment as a deterrent, and partly from the urge to dis-identify oneself as strongly as possible from the performers of these strangely attractive gestures of power.

It is possible, by rigorous searches and precautions, almost to eliminate the aircraft hijackings that caused such havoc in the late 1960s and early '70s. But there are many more ways in which the quasi-psychopath can hold society to ransom. I should not care to list them in detail, but if he is prepared to press home swiftly and ruthlessly, aware of the standard techniques that will be employed against him, the terrorist who is prepared to risk his own life can achieve a great deal against the ordinary citizen who is not. He can use selective or indiscriminate bombing and mining; he can use sniping, poisoning or kidnapping, against significant or innocent victims; he can use assassination, piracy, blackmail, forgery and vandalism. And he can be fiendishly cunning or mindlessly haphazard. This kind of terrorism is a young person's game, and it is disturbing to note that those who play it are getting younger and younger. There is also, through centres like Amsterdam, Rome, Paris and Beirut, increasing cooperation between revolutionary anarchist groups in different parts of the world: for example, the hiring of a Japanese suicide squad to carry out the Lydda Airport massacre for the Palestinians. As student travel continues to grow, so these contacts are likely to produce more and more bizarre alliances. And no target, however tender and innocent, will be spared by them.

And what is likely to be the future of individual violence? Even though Man is still evolving, he is not going to change his nature overnight. We are born 'wired' (to use Tiger and Fox's term[52]) for certain responses, some of which lead to violence, especially when we are taken out of our natural context, the small tribal pecking order, and flung into a huge conglomeration where our identity is constantly challenged. That is not to say that the solution to violence is to break society up into villages. There is plenty of violence in the villages of India, especially when rebels alarm the elders by attacking the established order. What we all need is to belong to a social unit which we can understand and in which we occupy a just position.

The future of violence in Britain and elsewhere depends to a large extent upon the achieving of a just society—where everyone gets, or believes that he gets, a fair chance to influence what happens to him, an opportunity to be placed and rewarded on his merits, and to be judged according to what he set out to do. Although we make periodic lurches towards it, such a society is far from being round the next corner. Recent surveys show the British to be surprisingly content with their family lives; but there is a disturbing resentment against the established political order, and a widespread feeling that ordinary people are powerless to influence the course of government. To a certain extent ordinary people do not really expect or want to tell the government precisely what it should do; but they would like to see what is being done on their behalf, more openly, and they would certainly like more chances to say what should *not* be done.

Again, while the schools and the mass media between them are steadily increasing the numbers of bright, able and well-informed citizens, the chances for them to find positions of leadership are becoming fewer rather than greater. There is now a move towards more self-government for Wales, Scotland and the English regions, which in principle is good; but at the levels on which most people identify themselves, the traditional boroughs, districts and parishes, not only power but social function is steadily drying up. Where once there was a squire, a vicar, a local publican and the village Bolshie, now there is the pub manager, the telly and a far-away council office. It is the lack of opportunity for advancement or meaningful occupation that drives ambitious youngsters out of the small towns and villages where they belong. If they can find no greater satisfaction in the cities, because authority has moved on once more to London or Brussels or Detroit, they may well be tempted to make themselves heard in acts of violence.

There is a good deal of evidence that violence is more easily provoked in conditions of overcrowding. The British are better than most people at working out social conventions to cope with this. But here again, the absence of opportunity to stand out, to identify oneself as an individual who matters, is liable to turn the inner city areas of Britain into replicas of the American ghettoes. Whether the inhabitants are Black, Catholic, Presbyterian or Muslim, the surest way of asserting one's will over them is to form a gang and intimidate them. In times of recession and loss of national confidence, the response to symptoms like these tends to be forceful repression rather than social reform. Repression only leads to more violence, and the cause of the trouble is left untreated.

I tried to make it clear earlier in this book that I do not believe violence has much to do with the examples currently set in the press and on the air. The mass media in a free society are part of the public bloodstream, the general circulation of ideas from which we all draw and to which we all contribute. We get those ideas from many more sources than television and the tabloid press. We observe the world around us with our own eyes and ears; we talk to each other in pubs and offices, ring each other up, write occasional letters, read and write books and argue with our children. In a free democracy we draw our own conclusions about what is going on. It is true that the mass media, like the wandering drolls and minstrels, regard it as part of their job to excite and entertain us as well as to pass on information. But news is what has changed; and today, because of the alliance between science and industry, things are changing so fast that older people resent having to make constant adjustments, while the young perhaps never have time to master anything completely. Unfairly, some of them blame the mass media, as if they had created these changes instead of merely reporting them. The mass media probably do help to speed some processes up—good ones as well as bad ones—but they are scarcely in a position to initiate very much. One of their first, most disturbing functions must be to act as a public warning system, and often the warnings are brutal.

Personally I believe that the public, including many responsible people who should know better, grossly overrate the influence of the press and broadcasting. Their power is very limited compared with that of real events and the people who control them. To maintain that the media should regard themselves as guilty until proved innocent, or be banned like dangerous drugs if it is even suspected that they might cause the slightest harm is not merely illiberal but dangerously irrelevant. Rather than treat Sunday newspaper sensations as if they were science, we should be learning how to build a sane society, how to recognise and heal sickness of mind before it damages others, and how to bring up whole and healthy children who will grow up to lead or to be led in a peace which must inevitably be strenuous, but need not be violent.

What then can we do about violence on its three levels? Are we sure that we really want to eliminate it, for a start?

At the root of everything lies the individual human conscience which tells us there are certain things we cannot do, because we are a certain type of person. This conscientious refusal to destroy one's image of oneself appears also in the group and the nation. So we cannot, as Raymond Aron puts it[6], deny states their right to be the ultimate judges of what the defence of their interests or their honour requires, just as we cannot deny individuals the right to protest and resist. In the first instance, resistance will almost certainly be verbal and conflict will take the form of argument: but one of the basic problems of violence today is that so many people have wearied of verbal argument. They claim that arguing is a waste of time which gets nobody anywhere. Debates between communist and non-communist are rendered pointless, it seems, by irreconcilable preconceptions. Arguments among democratic politicians are stultified by the tradition of scoring points off each other, by the refusal of either side to admit it could ever be wrong, by constant shifting of ground, evasion of issues and laying of conditions. Governments are overworked and lose patience: it is easier to shoot a man than persuade him. People and nations resort to violence because they have lost confidence in the power of reason, a faculty we have all helped to undermine.

Jose Moyane, commander of the African guerrillas in Portuguese Mozambique, told an interviewer: 'In the beginning we tried to negotiate. But when that failed, we were forced to fight for our freedom.' (I remember the Portuguese official in Goa telling me: 'Authority must be respected. Orders must be obeyed.') Camilo Torres, the Catholic priest who was killed fighting with the guerrillas in Colombia, wrote: 'Violence is not excluded from the christian ethic: the ethic is to be violent once and for all, in order to destroy the violence which the economic minorities exercise against the people.' 'Love that will not fight is not christian love,' added a conference of Latin American priests and laymen gathered during Allende's rule in Santiago, Chile.

The sad thing about these remarks, made so passionately from the heart, is that they are all built upon fallacies: the fallacy that violence can be controlled to achieve just the desired end, and the fallacy that one last stroke of violence will bring an end to violence. It is curious to find Catholic priests, of all people, subscribing to a Rousseauesque view of Man's perfectibility. Unfortunately, as Christ himself warned, those that live by the sword perish by it; and as W. B. Yeats observed, revolution only means that

'The beggars have changed places, but the lash goes on.'

It is clearly possible for christians to fight in good conscience, as they have managed to do for centuries under the doctrine of the Just War. But they should certainly not imagine they are fighting for christianity, which remains obstinately not of this world (that is, I believe, of the spirit rather than of political organisation). It is equally possible for christians, such as the Quakers, to refuse to fight, even though an oppressive and unchristian power may be said to gain advantage from their refusal. One must assume that such people would be doing their best non-violently to stem injustice, and would be prepared to suffer any consequences of opting out of the battle. But to rephrase what I said in an earlier chapter: if the military response to injustice is a gamble, so is the pacifist response. Governments are bound to play the gamble which the majority of their subjects support. Best of all is to avert the challenge in the first place, by far-sighted attention to foreign relations. Next best, in descending order, is to devise some form of international arbitration, to impose an international police discipline, or to limit and ritualise warfare so that it causes the least possible damage.

Far-sightedness in foreign affairs is a scarce commodity when governments have their work cut out running their countries from day to day, and when diplomats are regarded as an expensive luxury easily replaced by a telephone or an airline ticket. Yet most of the world's disputes are a long time coming to a head, are easy enough to spot for anyone who will take them seriously. Private research bodies like the Institute for Strategic Studies and the Institute for the Study of Conflict, in London, keep up a steady stream of reports on the potential trouble-spots. So indeed do the more serious newspapers, though the current philosophy and economics of their industry is tending to crowd out the old-style scholar-correspondent, who lived for years in his area and had the historical perspectives.

It should now be the purpose of the United Nations to maintain its own central registry of conflicts, to receive and investigate such reports as were made to it from reputable sources, to hold hearings on them and to refer any which it considered valid and pressing to the World Court or some specially constituted tribunal. Ideally, it should be made a condition of membership of the United Nations to accept this jurisdiction; just as it should become a condition of diplomatic relations between any two states that both should agree to refer any dispute to the United Nations system, and to accept its verdict upon pain of expulsion.

The United Nations should further create its own network of impartial conflict officers, each in charge of a particular area which he would regularly patrol and report upon. As a further precaution, the United Nations should operate its own system of reconnaissance satellites, so that no state could be entirely immune from surveillance, even if it refused to cooperate with the world organisation. To support this openness at other levels, member states would be required to give each other's newsmen and diplomats the widest freedom of movement and communication.

About the time when the Dutchman Grotius was publishing his proposals for humane warfare, a French monk, Émeric Crucé, was urging the establishment—in Venice—of an assembly of ambassadors and princes, pagan as well as christian, which might arbitrate in international disputes and, in the last resort, impose its verdicts by force. Thus the idea of intervention by the world community is far from new. What has helped to bedevil it all these years has been the confusion over whether to admit certain wars as just, and adopt an impartial position while the contenders fought it out according to the rules; or whether to treat all war as outlawed, and seek then to distinguish between the innocent victim, who should be aided, and the aggressor who should be punished. This later view came to the fore following the First World War. It may well be traced back to the concept of the *unjust* war, extended to the conclusion that since war was now so hideous, all wars must be unjust. The view was incorporated into the so-called Kellogg Pact of 1928, under which (to no avail) more than sixty nations eventually condemned and renounced war as a solution for international problems, and it was revived once more in the Charter of the United Nations. The earlier Covenant of the League of Nations was less ambitious: its signatories bound themselves not to resort to war in any dispute until the various processes of the League had been exhausted, and even then to allow a three-month cooling-off period before taking up arms. Sanctions and military intervention were provided for against those who broke the Covenant.

But through the entire system there ran, as there runs today, the difficult question: who is the aggressor? The answer is seldom clear-cut, even when it may seem so on the battlefield. Provocation, subversion, obstinacy and insolence are not unknown in relations between states, as we have seen in the Middle East, South-east Asia and the Indo-Pakistan subcontinent. Yet the moralistic insistence that the supposed aggressor has no rights, must not be allowed any benefit from his act, or even to appear on the same footing as his supposedly innocent victim, has frustrated the solution of one conflict after another. That is not to say there is *never* an innocent victim: it would be hard, for example, to say what Holland had done to deserve the German invasion of 1940. But in most cases, the

blame for an outbreak of war ought to be shared, and it is
foolish and unjust to insist that peace be restored purely upon
the basis of going back to Square One.

So long as the United Nations endeavours to settle disputes
by moral-political voting in the Security Council and the
General Assembly, instead of through international arbitration
and mediation using a courts system, it will be impossible to
get settlements objectively enforced. And enforcement machinery there clearly must be, beginning with fines, diplomatic
sanctions and expulsion and rising through trade and financial
embargoes to military occupation. At the Disarmament Conference of 1932, France proposed an international police force
to which the great powers should assign all their most lethal
weapons like heavy bombers, tanks and artillery. Thirty or
forty years later, Liddell Hart and Leonard Beaton were both
proposing a world force to which nuclear weapons should be
surrendered. Ever since 1947, the Military Staff Committee of
the United Nations has had the blueprint of a standing U.N.
Force. International expeditionary forces raised *ad hoc* have
done useful work in the Middle East, the Congo and Cyprus.
But it becomes steadily harder to find nations whose forces are
acceptable to those in conflict, while it is steadily clearer that a
permanent force owing allegiance solely to the Secretary
General, with island bases round the world, and supported by
some form of United Nations revenue (for example, a small tax
on international transport) is needed to deal swiftly with
emergencies. In order to ensure that such a force was not
constantly being called out to protect corrupt tyrannies against
their own subjects, it would have to be a condition of United
Nations intervention that any government requesting it must
submit the whole dispute to the world arbitration system.

The machinery I have outlined would have its defects—the
surrender of national sovereignty it requires would have to be
matched by some form of popular involvement in the vast
United Nations structure. But it would go further than the
existing United Nations mechanism in 'encapsulating conflicts'—a detestable but useful term devised by the sociologist
Amitai Etzioni[18] to describe a process of smothering a potentially dangerous situation in a vast ritual of debate, consultation
and conference. Even now a good deal of steam can be let out

of a crisis by summoning the Security Council, calling summit conferences and dispatching special envoys hither and thither. Once a conflict has been modified and confined—'encapsulated' —in a rigmarole of this kind, leaders feel they are doing something constructive, tempers cool down and everyone becomes involved in the game almost for its own sake. The very abstractness of the United Nations headquarters building, and its remoteness from most of the issues being discussed there help to eliminate passion. You do not, it was once remarked, have to establish universal love to get peace between nations. It is only necessary to dissuade them from fighting each other.

It might seem obvious that the best way of doing this was to get the nations to disarm, even the 'general and complete disarmament' proposed by the Soviet Union in its more intoxicated moments. This seems to me much less important than the steps I have already outlined, with the single exception— hardly to be expected, unfortunately, of totalitarian states—of abolishing conscription. The menace of large standing armies, their generals restlessly planning things for them to do, needs to be emphasised far more than it usually is. Could the Pentagon, for example, ever have contemplated the escalation of the Vietnam War without the draft system? However, that apart, we must admit that over the past thirty years the ultimate armament, the nuclear deterrent, really has deterred the final catastrophe of a Third World War. It has done so not because either superpower has kept an inhibiting lead over the other, but because the two have remained neck and neck. Neither can be sure that, even if it were the first to press the red button, the other side's capacity to strike back would not leave both defeated. Agreements on the limitation of strategic arms are more in the nature of economy measures than real disarmament. Indeed the sheer expense of modern weapons and their maintenance may eventually price some of the worst extravagance off the market.

There are many better uses for money than Multiple Independent Re-entry Vehicles (or MIRVs), and the fewer that are made the better for all of us. But more important for the stability of peace all over the world is the limitation of *conventional* arms, the jets, tanks, rockets and gunboats which nowadays can rush from country to country with the speed of a jumbo freightlifter. An outright ban on the trafficking of arms would be of little use, even if it were observed by the major arms-producing countries. Industrialised nations would soon purchase blueprints and produce their own, and the less developed would patronise the second-hand arms dealers and the smugglers. What needs to be imposed by the United Nations is a system of licensing and inspection for all nations: for this country, so many tanks and aircraft, so many thousand men, according to its frontiers, resources, population and neighbours. Groups of neighbouring states could be brought together and their quotas worked out in consultation with each other. From time to time, local situations would be reviewed, quotas revised and licences (issued for large fees, to the benefit of U.N. development funds) revoked or increased. It would even be worth calculating and publishing the figures—actual as well as authorised—for states which declined to cooperate in the scheme. It would be embarrassing for a foreign minister whose assessed need was fifty jet fighters to face a General Assembly which had good reason to believe he had more than five hundred. For what? delegates would demand to know.

The United Nations secretariat, in conjunction with the Red Cross, ought also to take the initiative to bring war back within civilised bounds. It should seek to ensure the immunity of civilians and civil installations from ground attack and aerial bombing, the humane treatment of prisoners (now neglected or exploited) and the innocence of crops, animals and private property. Certain weapons, starting with nuclear warheads and extending through gas, germs and napalm to pellet-bombs and poisoned bullets should once more be proscribed as inhuman. It seems hardly likely that Man will ever go back to the days of chivalry, with no fighting at weekends and combat only with one's social equals, but is it wholly impossible that when fighting does break out between two parties of limited resources, they might agree to limit it to certain times and places, or to conduct it under United Nations auspices, if U.N. mediation had failed? The object would be to ritualise and encapsulate the proceedings, until they became something approaching a mediaeval tournament. No doubt it would all be televised live to the world, and no doubt there would follow an outcry against the revival of gladiatorial games. If the whole thing were then suppressed, so much the better—or would it be?

It has been suggested[49] that the United Nations should institute a wide range of athletic, cultural and scientific contests, which would serve as outlets for national competitiveness and thus as a substitute for war. Certainly it is worth trying, and it might even be extended to factory and farm production. But it is even more important, in my view, that the United Nations should encourage the commercial interlocking of states with conflicting political systems. For example, the more the United States and the Soviet Union come to rely on each other for grain and machinery on the one hand, timber and natural gas on the other, the less they can afford to go to war. This may seem to contradict what I have already said about the dangers of becoming too reliant upon external sources of supply, and about how a threat to one's sources may provoke a warlike response. But the point is to achieve a *mutual* dependence, not one-sided. The danger in the Arabs' use of the oil weapon in 1973 was that we needed them a great deal more than they needed us. In short, there must be far greater equality between nations. The developed world will have to pay infinitely higher prices to the underdeveloped while developing peoples like the Arabs must subsidise those lower down the ladder, the Asians and Africans.

Finally, in our efforts to avoid violence between nations, we should pay a good deal more attention to the selection of our leaders, and those who advise them. A British Prime Minister today might fairly complain of being too power*less*; but in fact, in an emergency, power is still concentrated into remarkably few hands. And we have only to think back to the Suez invasion to realise how important it is for those in power to be in the best of mental and physical health. Any government should have an independent medical adviser, appointed by the nation's professional medical association, to examine those in responsible positions at regular intervals and report any signs of breakdown or strain. If some leading businesses do this already, how much more so should governments?

It also seems to me important that our leaders should take regular rest and recreation, and that instead of jeering at them for golfing, sailing or shooting grouse, we should sigh with relief that they are not working themselves stupid at Number

Ten or the White House. It will probably be argued that we expect too much of our rulers for them to be able to work the forty-hour weeks the rest of us demand. I would reply that if shorter hours meant they had to appoint more assistants and delegate more of their personal work, so much the better. What we have to escape from is the tight cabal that never goes any-where or meets anyone and eventually becomes a society in its own right. If, as the UNESCO Charter has it, 'Wars begin in the minds of men', we must see to it that the minds are well-balanced. Looking back over quite recent history, the capacity of the most able of men to justify their own mistakes and pur-sue them *ad absurdum* seems inexhaustible. While we certainly need moral dedication, we must also remember that the dead-liest of the sins is Pride: even the proud conviction that one's own moral sense is infallible.

So I believe it is important for most people not to become wedged into a single, self-justifying rut. We should change our occupations from time to time, and that is particularly vital for those in authority. I shall return to it later in this chapter, but it seems to me specially unhealthy for politicians—who are by their very calling aggressive men—to live nothing but politics. They should return periodically to some occupation shared by their constituents, or at least take sabbaticals in the universities.

What can we do to lessen violence between groups, to elimi-nate terrorism and civil wars? It so happens that I am typing these words on December 18, 1973, a day which has seen two major acts of violence: the burning to death of twenty-nine innocent passengers at Rome Airport by a squad of Palestinian terrorists—and the injuring of fifty-two passers-by in a West-minster street, by an IRA car-bomb. There is limitless scope here for moral outrage. These were gestures as fatuous as they were cruel, irrelevant to the problems of Ireland, Palestine or anywhere else, calculated only to give a sadistic orgasm to those who perpetrated them. Perhaps the casualties might have been reduced by smarter police work; though I cannot see that even giving warning that a bomb has been planted purges an act of terrorism of its sin, or transfers the blame to anyone else. What these outrages really have to teach us is that, in a free society, the terrorist can always get through to commit his crime. The Rome Airport gang defeated the metal detectors by producing their guns as they approached the checkpoint and shooting their way through it to the aircraft. Some months earlier, another gang had been arrested as it was preparing to use anti-aircraft rockets of advanced design to shoot down an approaching Israeli airliner. There are advances in terrorism yet to come.

What the free world has to realise is that, if it wants to remain free, it will, besides maintaining police vigilance, have to accept civilian casualties. Sooner or later someone will have to give the order to assault a hijacked plane, hostages or no hostages—refuse to release convicted terrorists, whatever the blackmail—turn down demands for aviation fuel, whether or not the plane is blown up in retaliation. If innocent hostages are killed—well, there can never be any adequate solace in any kind of bereavement. But the free world should honour those victims as martyrs in the cause of freedom, and see that their dependants are taken care of even more generously than those of soldiers who fall in battle. Those are hard words to write; but this is the knot of the problem: if men are ready to die for what is wrong, how can the right triumph unless its supporters are ready to die too?

As with war it is, of course, far better to see that the conflict does not arise in the first place. Many Palestinians have undoubtedly had a valid grievance, even if it was not against those they made to suffer. More dangerous still, there has been no effective power structure up which able young Palestinians could climb, even no country with which they could identify themselves. I do not think the killer squads have had the slightest moral case for saying that the World Community must bear the responsibility for what they do: that is like a child holding a vase over its head and saying, 'Unless you give me what I want, *you* are responsible for this vase getting broken.' But in terms of practical self-interest, there are things the World Community could and should have done to head off this kind of trouble. As in the case of conflict between nations, the makings of guerrilla violence are usually in clear view long before the first acts are committed. It takes no great imagination to see the trouble that continental Europe is

building up for itself in the form of 'guest workers' from Turkey
and North Africa, or the United States among poor Mexican
labour, or Britain in the shape of undigested lumps of Asian
and Caribbean immigration. It is unjust nonsense for Englishmen to talk about 'sending the blacks back where they came
from' when more and more of them come from the same
English cities as ourselves. Their parents were imported by
economic demand as surely as the African slaves were imported
into the British North American colonies two or three centuries
ago. We English have a long tradition of dealing in flesh.
(Though I doubt if our record is as bad as that of Spain, which
succeeded in reducing the population of Mexico from twenty-
five million to one million within a century.)

It is hardly surprising that many immigrants to Britain do
not try very hard to integrate with a community which admits
them to do its dirty work but shows no sign of welcoming them.
Asians in particular protect themselves against the blows of
fate with a strong extended family system; but they see nothing
to replace that in our society. So, like anyone else outnumbered
in strange surroundings, like the British sahibs in India, they
try to maintain as much of their familiar identity, their food,
clothing and customs, as they can. The majority community
instinctively resents this: not only are these strangers from outside the territory, but apparently our ways are not good enough
for them—can it be we are not as splendid as we thought?
Impossible! It's an insult!

I have already suggested that black, brown and yellow
British can provide us with a bridge to the Afro-Asian world,
with which we must come to terms for the sake of the world's
peace. I have also pointed out that they only came here because
our economy demanded them. We might remember three or
four other points: that in admitting these immigrants we might
claim to be making a small contribution towards sharing our
fortune with the Third World; that we in our time have
claimed the right to settle freely all over Asia and Africa; that
the mixture and intermarriage of different cultures has usually
had a stimulating effect on civilisation; and that in any case
the British Race—which some are so eager to protect—will be
what our children and grandchildren choose to make it, not
what we attempt to impose on them. Personally I do not think

we shall be free of interracial strife until miscegenation is wide-spread and unremarkable.

But both sides must make an effort if we are to break up the foundations now being laid for violent conflict. The immigrant would be wise to overcome some of his inhibitions against inviting strangers into his home and making friends of them. The native Briton must try to understand the immigrant's way of life and to see that it is not a rival to his own, simply an alternative. I have heard it well argued by Indian friends that as well as broadcasts in Hindi explaining Britain to the immigrants, there should be even more broadcasts in English explaining the immigrants to the British. Our schools, too, should cultivate respect for the different religions and cultures in our country. Somehow conformity must be made unfashionable and membership of a minority something to be proud of.

I am also convinced that discrimination against colour is something that should be actively prosecuted. It may not be possible to make people virtuous by law; but what virtue is in fact practised if the law lends no support to it? There was a good deal of scoffing at 'token integration' and the 'front office nigger' in the United States; but it took a few tokens to break the ice. After that it was found that Negroes did actually have merits of their own to be judged on.

But what about purely political violence—terrorism and urban guerrilla activity? (As I type these words, the Spanish Prime Minister has just been assassinated by a mine under his car.) I believe, for a start, that governments do have an absolute right and duty these days to be as ingenious against subversion as the subversives are against them. Naturally I maintain there should be no question whatever of torture or brutality —and here I cannot draw a line between physical cruelty and the use of sensory deprivation, sleeplessness, total isolation and other, swifter techniques. Any security force which indulges in any of these practices is striking a blow for the other side, which, in its turn, will surely be using them. But a security force would betray its trust if it failed to set up the deepest possible network of agents and paid informers among those elements known to favour the violent overthrow of government. And those who do so conspire have little right to object if they in turn find themselves subverted.

There is no denying that all this could open the way to a political police force or an outbreak of the Watergate Capers. But I can only speak for democracy (where it can be argued that the mere existence of a standing army *could* lead to a military dictatorship). The important points are that counter-subversion must remain strictly in the hands of the police, that they must proceed solely against criminal (not political) offences, and that a democratic parliament must remain vigilant at all times in the defence of civil liberty.

But it is even more important that the parliament show itself responsive to the needs of the public; that it should act promptly when called upon, and that its legitimacy should be beyond question. One of the difficulties here is that while responsiveness and legitimacy call for more frequent elections than we in Britain usually get—say, once every two or three years—it is almost impossible for an administration to master a situation and produce effective results in so short a time. We expect too much too soon. I should not care to propose a solution in a paragraph or two, but clearly it must involve abandoning the crude two-party adversary system which Britain has kept for so long, and adopting a more subtle, continuous process of coalition and compromise. Proportional representation would be part of this, and our democracy would then be able to offer the voter a choice of independent candidates and regional as well as national parties which would be much more likely to serve his particular interests and capture his loyalty. If the present system must continue, I believe that at the very least we should make voting compulsory (as it is in Australia) but that the ballot paper should carry the option to vote, in effect, 'a plague on both (or all) your houses'. The established parties might find the results very sobering.

At present, it seems to me, the average voter is disillusioned by the enormous gap between what politicians promise and what they are able to deliver. Voters are also fed up with the endless game of verbalising, in which each party claims virtue for itself and attributes vice to the others. Under a coalition system, at least one other party would have to be granted some share of virtue and politicians would begin to paint each other in human shades of grey, rather than demonic black and angelic white. But so long as a British government can rely on party discipline to ensure the loyalty of its MPs, it can continue to pretend that no other view but its own need be taken seriously. With constant debate along those lines in the mass media, it is little wonder that the public loses interest in rational discussion and either lapses into apathy or responds to emotional appeals.

Man, being a mixed creature, is incapable of action without some emotional justification. But reason must come first, and emotion be aroused by the revelations of reason. To put the process the other way round—to begin with a passion and then try to find justification for it—is precisely Hitler's way. It is therefore extremely important that all of us should respect the laws of logical, creative discussion, that our children should be taught what it means to be objective and how they should see through the deceits and fallacies of commercial and political propaganda.

Neither businessmen nor politicians should arouse expectations they cannot fulfil. Ultimately they are debasing the language to the point where it can no longer be accepted as the currency of communication and only force will serve to convey a meaning. Often one hears it said during an election campaign, 'My friends, let us debate the issues—not the personalities.' So be it. But with debate defective, and the issues apparently beyond control, who can blame the public for concluding that the personalities are what really matter? Certainly the honesty and achievement of the candidate are important. But personality is the hardest thing of all to debate, and it is not always exposed by television. In the end, there is no substitute for meeting the man face to face.

The whole purpose of a responsive democratic system is, it seems to me, to avert the need for violence by ensuring that social justice is available for the asking. But, as Toynbee observes[54], we cannot have social justice without curbing somebody's liberty. Democracy, he says, is a smokescreen to conceal the conflict between liberty and equality, which only fraternity can reconcile. But how can anyone believe that he has fifty million—or five thousand million—brothers? The ancient answer, which still serves some of us today, is: by accepting the Fatherhood of God. But for most the answer must lie through the more strenuous process of getting to know and

understand other groups and their ways of life. Achieving that
is very far from simple. Even catholics and protestants living
for years on opposite sides of the same Belfast street can still
regard each other as aliens. Educational exchanges of pre-teen
children leave only the shallowest of impressions which soon
wash out; older students are too often kept at home by national
exam demands which cannot be reconciled with those of other
countries. I should like to see at least six months of study abroad
a compulsory part of any first degree. Tourism is of very little
use in getting peoples to understand one another. The average
foreign tourist never enters a single ordinary home or speaks
to anybody except waiters, guides and souvenir sellers. The
only way to get to understand other people is to work along-
side them. But few people want to uproot themselves for anything more lasting than a week or two on a sunny beach. Mass
migrations would too easily produce the very antagonisms we
are trying to avoid. Nevertheless within organisations like the
European Community, and through the agency of corres-
ponding bodies like the churches, industries and professional
organisations, some system of working exchanges could, I
think, be devised.

There are obviously better chances for social engineering
within a nation. The term is not an attractive one, I agree;
but what needs to be done is really no more brutal or illiberal
than the suppression of slavery, the regulation of factory labour,
the introduction of free education, health services and adult
suffrage were in their days. Most of what is needed is a good
deal less terrifying than the graduated income-tax. And fundamentally what is needed is an educational system which will
encourage not just equality but fraternity, among classes,
among groups, among regions. Within Britain it should be
relatively easy for children from Glasgow to spend a month or
two at school in Cornwall, or for Essex children to spend a
month or two in Wales. We can press ahead with the creation
of a truly public system before which the private system will
largely wither away or wish to integrate itself voluntarily.
Personally I believe private schools to be socially disruptive,
psychologically damaging and economically past justifying.
Perhaps selective taxation, like taxes on other luxuries, might
help them on their way. But I do not think it right brutally to

suppress them, any more than it would have been to suppress
Oxford and Cambridge. A gradual but steady transformation
is needed.

It would be naive to pretend that equality is the whole
solution to the problem of social violence. Provided there is a
genuine sense of fraternity and fairness people are prepared to
tolerate a wider range of *in*equality than they otherwise would.
I think it is obvious, though, that in Britain and most other
western nations the range of privileges and rewards is far too
wide for an increasingly thoughtful and well-informed people
to tolerate. It is an illusion (though an attractive leftist myth)
that by lopping off the income of the top ten percent and
redistributing it among the workers we could all eat caviar for
tea. Apparently astronomical salaries are made nonsense of by
the tax system in any case; it would make better sense if both
the salaries and the upper tax brackets were lower. However,
multi-thousand-pound salaries do create handy myths for
revolutionaries to exploit; it seems foolish to assist them. More
to the point, there must be a closing-up of the pay differentials
between skilled and unskilled workers and between workers
and professional people. It would be better if this could be
achieved by a conservative or social democratic administration,
whose leadership would be accepted by middle-class people
with a minimum of resistance. For it to be imposed by a
government of the extreme left could be appallingly destructive.

Industrial violence is something that has bothered Britain
less than most countries; which is why, when it does occur, it
bothers us considerably. Just as a good deal of civil violence is
the result of stupidity and lack of foresight by those in authority,
and just as many wars could have been averted if governments
had not assumed that sleeping dogs would lie for ever, so a
great deal of industrial disruption results from the failure of
managements to manage skilfully, to pay as much attention to
personnel relations as they do to sales and production—in a
nutshell, to realise that the average worker has a bigger stake
in the business than the average shareholder. The shareholder
can easily enough take his money elsewhere. The worker, in
today's Britain, too often has nowhere else to go. His refusal or
inability to move away from his home ground is a source of

national stability and of frustration, too. Some form of em-
ployees' participation in management must come to every
workplace in Britain, and it seems to me that it should be built
into the workers' duties, requiring compulsory attendance and
voting at whatever councils are devised. If the trade unions
really *are* running the country, then the response surely should
be for us all to form and join our unions—which would not
necessarily all be left-wing socialist—and for the unions to
learn what management responsibilities really are.

In short, we have been talking for three or four generations
now about how liberal parliamentary democracy, or social
democracy, was going to realise the ancient ideals of liberty,
equality and fraternity, without bloodshed. Evolution rather
than Revolution was the promise. It seems to me, with a kind
of siege economy closing in on us, our past extravagance and
over-indulgence catching up on us, and a J-curvaceous outlook
for many who have had such continually rising expectations,
that our democracy had better start delivering the goods a
great deal more rapidly than it has done, or bloodshed will not
be the stranger in our streets that it has been for the best part
of a century. Once blood does flow and martyrs are made, the
revolutionary myth will be there to take fire, consuming the
just and the unjust together. As a first step towards averting
this, politicians and journalists in particular must exercise a
new responsibility towards the language, and cease to use it
either as a medium of mere entertainment or a sport for scoring
points off one's opponents. If violence takes over where language
breaks down, then the process of free, constructive discussion
must be exercised with far greater respect for accuracy and
reason, lest the whole meaning of language be destroyed and
leave no alternative but blows.

But we must not deceive ourselves about the effectiveness of
the political process. Violence is not simply the product of
social misorganisation. Man has made himself a world in which
he is a misfit; but in a just world and a just society there would
still be violence, because of the very nature of Man: part angel
and part animal, part solitary and part comrade, part adult
and part child, part free and part conditioned—a creature
driven upwards by the fury of dissent. And while conflict is the
very condition of Man's supremacy, like the tools he has in-

vented it is the instrument both of construction and destruction. Man's ambition to assert himself not only provokes conflict but requires it. He demands challenge and resistance in order to assure himself that he exists independently and that his existence is recognised by others. A totally compliant world would be no more satisfying than a dream. Any brave new world that we devise must provide challenge and permit rebellion.

As Lorenz remarked, people are terrified of exposing Man's free will as nothing but an illusion: as if the least concession to determinism would bring the whole edifice of free will crashing to the ground. Of course we have freedom of choice, but not at all levels all the time. We still have instinctive patterns of behaviour wired up in our minds and ready to be stimulated by experience. If we really were, by nature, the dangerous animals we seem to be, we would certainly have become equipped by now with rituals to prevent ourselves destroying each other. The fact that we are not so equipped shows, not that we were wired for murder, but that the consequences of our free conceptual thinking have got far ahead of any wiring. Because of this we have allowed (for example) our numbers to multiply to an extent where it is extremely hard for us to know and love our multitudinous neighbours. We have devised remote, impersonal ways of killing which eliminate the occasions for pity which the spectacle of one human being in distress naturally arouses in another. Worse still, we have devised tricks of thought which enable us to depersonalise even those whom we should normally regard as our brothers and sisters.

Is there no health in us? On the contrary, if Man will only give himself a fair chance there is a great deal of health in him. No species is wired for its own destruction, or it would not be with us today. We are, besides being a clever and ambitious species, a uniquely cooperative species, a creative species and even a loving species. Not even the ants collaborate constructively on as widespread a scale as Man. Not even the birds devise beauty for its own sake as we do. No other creature will voluntarily give help to a stranger in need. Man murders, Man riots and Man goes to war, it is true. But he also nurses his sick and elderly to the very end, taxes himself to house the helpless and poor, and brings relief in time of disaster to people thousands of miles away who are of totally different tongues and

colours. Perhaps we have such a low opinion of ourselves because
our information media spend too much time on the few score
members of the Provisional IRA and too little on the thousands
who work for charities like OXFAM, Freedom From Hunger,
Shelter and Help the Aged. A week or two spent reporting
their activities gives one a less desperate view of Man's capa-
bilities.

If each of us looks into himself, he will realise that he does
not in fact *wish* to hate, fight or destroy for its own sake. It is
no mere excuse to say, like the Ulster housewife, that we are
driven to it. We are constantly driven, as we acknowledge,
against our better nature. We are driven by failure of communication, failure of understanding.

I must repeat: every act of violence *says* something, even if,
like the vandalism committed by some urban lout, it is nothing
more specific than, 'I never asked to come here—I hate this
place and it hates me', or, 'What else can I do to make *them*
feel I'm here?' Nobody really wants to feel like that, and punishment, as we are slowly coming to recognise, is no answer to it.
My response to anyone who cares to call me a bleeding-heart
do-gooder is: but what are we trying to achieve? To show how
virtuous *we* are in comparison with the criminal, or to stop his
offence from being repeated and to make a more useful and
contented citizen of him? What puzzles me about advocates
of strict law-and-order is how expensive and inefficient their
methods seem to be. There certainly are some dangerous offen-
ders—urban guerrillas among them—who must be segregated
from society and for whom some sort of prison is inevitable.
But for the most part, imprisonment at more than forty pounds
a week is an expensive way of failing to do what can only be
achieved in normal surroundings; namely to adapt the offender
to the life he must share with his fellow beings. If he owes
reparation to society, he should pay it—and earn it. But there
is no sense, and very little justice, in punishing his family as
well as himself by removing the offender to a place where he
can earn nothing for anyone and carry out none of his social
responsibilities. What we need is not more prisons and warders
but more probation officers, psychiatric social workers, social
workers and criminal psychiatrists. And we need to place their
services much higher on the pay scale than we do at present.

The need for more mental health workers and education in mental health seems to me vital to the treatment of individual violence, if not quite central to it. In his last, neglected work, *Island*, Aldous Huxley sets out many ideas that bear upon this. Every intellectual in his (alas, doomed) Utopia must also do some physical task, to make him a whole man. Every child belongs to a Mutual Adoption Club of fifteen or twenty-five assorted couples who adopt each other and their children in a kind of flexible extended family. Any love of power that shows itself in the individual (including, no doubt, what Christopher Serpell has called the politician's *morbus politicus*—the belief that he knows best what's good for his fellows) is deflected away from people and on to things. And the growing child undergoes careful psychological monitoring to spot any maladjustment before it does damage. Why not? We do as much for the child's body. Perhaps we hesitate to watch as carefully over their minds for several reasons, none of which does us any honour. The first is the expense, the second our outmoded shame at confessing to mental distress, and the third is our long neglect of mental health in general.

Even now, psychology and psychiatry are in their infancy—though I must gratefully add that few infants have made such progress in relatively so short a time. The proper study of mankind really is Man. Yet we still, as laymen anyway, barely know who we are, let alone how to bring up and educate our children. I once said this to a very superior establishment person, who replied haughtily that Charterhouse and Oxford were quite good enough for *his* children, thank you. . . . It seemed hardly worth the time to explain he had missed my point. Our ignorance begins at the very beginning. To give only a few examples: we do not really *know* (not well enough to practise) what role the father should play in birth and infancy, how much the baby should be in physical contact with a parent, whether bottle-feeding is something to be actively discouraged, whether mothers should be dissuaded from going out to work for some years, how other adults and children should be introduced into a baby's life, how far the infant should be stimulated and how far kept quiet, how and when it should be taught what, and how parents should respond to the perennial challenge of crying and tantrums and showing off. We guess and we consult our instincts and our garbled experience. But our lives as parents are overcrowded with other things; the devices we have invented to help us with our labours have simply enabled us to cram three days' problems into one. For the most part we are groping hurriedly in the dark. If we do our job as parents surprisingly well, it is not surprising that we turn out too many personalities that are monstrous or crippled for life.

We waste much time in our schools teaching children things which they are slow to learn, because they do not see the point of them, either because they are poorly taught or because the children do not yet need them. They will learn such things fast enough if and when they are required. Instead, we should be teaching them what they can immediately apply: understanding of themselves and of ourselves, so that they will understand why the class bully bullies, why boys and girls seem 'the same only different' mentally, why teenagers clash with parents, what are normal problems and irritations and what are serious mental disorders, and why parents who love their children also hurt them—and the other way round. At a higher level, our children should also learn to understand and respect members of other groups and minorities than their own, to comprehend racism and intolerance, and to tell the difference between fact and fantasy in politics and advertising. They should learn to see the dangers behind the popular myths, and the human frailties of popular heroes. And along with the art of rational analysis and discussion, they should learn sympathy and tolerance. They should learn what it is to be human.

And to be human is to be less desperate in the pursuit of affection from others than we commonly suppose. Being ambitious to assert rather than to submit ourselves, our primary need is to *give* love rather than to receive it. This is perhaps the greatest open secret about Mankind, but one which each of us has to learn in his or her own very personal way. What the world needs now is not just love, sweet love, as the song puts it; it needs opportunities to *express* love, and thus to be asserted as loving, so that we can confidently love ourselves.

At the root of the depressive mental illness which gnaws through the western world lies a terrible fear of being exposed as violently unloving, and therefore, incidentally, as unlovable. For this, the punishment which we inflict upon ourselves is a ball and chain of guilt, or a sense of being hounded like a criminal, so heavy that, too often, only self-inflicted death can remove it. No one who has not fled before it, year after darkening year, can appreciate its hopelessness and its terror.

Once again, it all seems to begin at the very beginning, and those who are fortunate enough to have escaped it—the majority, I hope—have my congratulations on being unable to follow the trail back. To the infant, the mother is everything peaceful, loving and secure, everything that reassures his earliest doubts about his place in the world. But she is also the source of his earliest frustrations, a persistent barrier to his emotions, the cause of his first feelings of hatred, aggression and violence. How can this conflict be resolved? How can the hated authority be also the loving mother, the Creator be also the Destroyer? The baby cannot reason out a sophisticated explanation. He cannot communicate by language at all and even such violence as he can command is ineffectual. He may even attribute to his mother the violence he feels towards her—the beginning of the psychological process of self-deception or Projection. But since the baby is utterly dependent upon the mother's love for survival, he must submit to her authority, thrust down his unreasoning resentment and gradually accept the *moral* view that is is wicked to entertain feelings of violence towards those in authority who say they love us—and may indeed love us. There is no violence more destructive than that between lover and beloved.

What is essential in order to overcome this nightmare tangle of dark, unreasoning emotions is understanding; understanding of the *needs* that every individual has and shares with others; understanding that can only be achieved through a process in which terms like wicked and virtuous have no use. We must understand why we are what we are; why others are what they are. We must clear away the misunderstandings and projections that lie between us, and thus achieve love and forgiveness—not only of each other, but each of himself or herself.

Most of it is there in the gospels already. But the white Anglo-Saxon protestant brand of organised christianity, with its brooding emphasis on sin and its embarrassed vagueness about love, is of little comfort to those who need its help most. Official

christianity dwells obsessively upon our wickedness and un-
worthiness. It implies that if we have any good points at all we
deserve no credit for them, but should ascribe it to a God who
appears to be above and beyond us, rather than within us. I am
well aware that some christians will assure me their interpretation is otherwise, that they have always listened for 'that of God
which is in all of us'. I only wish I, and many others, had met
them earlier. Pauline christianity as preached in Britain for
centuries past almost deserves a less vicious form of Nietzsche's
criticism: it has frowned too heavily upon the joy and fun and
goodness of human life. It has, above all, missed the implication
of the commandment that we should love our neighbour *as
ourselves*. For unless we can love, forgive and accept ourselves
first of all, it is futile to attempt to devote our love to others. A
broken reed can prop up nothing.

Our feelings of guilt are made no lighter by the Anglo-
Saxon tendency to bundle into one shapeless bag marked Love
a wide range of affections, all the way from sexual passion
through friendship and fellowship to charity and goodwill, a
range that a more learned christianity has been able to distinguish under such headings as *eros*, *agapee*, *philia* and *caritas*.
The divisions between them are hardly watertight. But the
different aspects of love, by other names, make perfect sense to
most of us. Homosexuality upsets my stomach; but I find it
sad that good christians seem to hold back from deep friendship
because they find it embarrassing, perhaps fearful lest a gesture
of affection be interpreted as sexual; or that they turn away
from the widest goodwill towards men, because they feel themselves incapable of 'loving all mankind'. Because of our shame
over sex, we have muffled the discussion of love which would
enable us to appreciate its variety.

There is love in abundance in all normal people; certainly
enough to prevent the aggressive ambition in us from becoming
destructive. It is saddest of all that, too often, we fail to bring
up our children with sufficient opportunity for expressing their
natural affection—that we even infect them with inhibitions
against showing it. The urge to show love is why young people
crave romantic pop songs, and why, at an earlier age, they need
dolls, teddy bears and—best of all—pet animals, as outlets, as
exercises, for their love. Personally, I should not care to live in

a commune. At my age I am fussy about my privacy and I do not fancy the squalor, seediness and malnutrition that seem to go with the simple life. But commune life is an attempt to widen the opportunities for affection; and I do believe that, like the people in *Island*, we should be trying to create a less fractioned, more integrated way of life for our children. By which I mean the integration of life between the sexes (so far as is natural), between the three generations of the family (without being authoritarian), between families, and between the stages into which our lives have become chopped up.

Modern Man has his life arbitrarily divided into education, work and retirement. Where one begins, another leaves off never to return. How much more rewarding all those processes would be if they were interleaved: so that children could get some idea of what doing a job was while they were still at school; so that young people could, if they wished, move to and fro between higher education and a variety of occupations and experiments; and so that an older person might (for example) go back to college at thirty, start teaching at forty, retire for a year at fifty, then begin a new career before going back to college for a doctorate and becoming a priest at sixty-five. Organising such a pattern of life would be far from simple, nor would it suit everybody. Perhaps those who opted for it would need the services of an agent or manager to find the right vacancies and even out the fluctuations in income. But the system would avoid the meaningless dead-ends and the long, deep ruts to which the present compartmented way of life condemns so many of us. Where there was hope and challenge and meaning in life, there would also be less provocation to violence.

What, though, is to give our life this purpose, this meaning? If it is simply to be the objective of staying alive as long and as comfortably as possible, showing no more than conventional benevolence to our neighbour in the hope that he will return the favour to us, then sooner or later almost any means, including violence, will be claimed as justifiable by the end. Once again: unless our ultimate good really is ultimate, we shall go wildly astray. Furthermore, there will remain in most of us an unsatisfied yearning after something higher and wider than our own personal advantage. That it is the Party, the Nation or the Class is a less than ultimate substitute that can only be maintained by enforcing an intellectually narrow regime. For the free soul, the yearning is after something that cannot be described in finite terms, something to which poetry, music and the other arts come closer, because they can still communicate when prosaic words fail and where force is irrelevant: something in us and of us and around us that—in an effort to explain ourselves to ourselves—we have called God. I certainly do not know any better term, unless it be Christ, and I do not know of any better context for either than the christian gospels. Like the Holy City itself, they have been fought over, devastated, restored, exploited and developed almost beyond recognition. And yet there remains in them a faith with no spiritual alternative for most of us raised in the European tradition—and many beyond.

Its message is as compact and full of energy as a nuclear warhead, but with the very opposite impact: we are to make peace within ourselves, we are to love one another *as* ourselves, we are to accept God as Man and not other than Man, and realise that whatever the political group or nation may do, the ultimate answer of the spirit to violence must be endurance, suffering and—if need be—martyrdom. To repeat myself once again: if violence can recruit its martyrs, so must righteousness. This is the barest outline of the message as I understand it. There is a great deal more massed beyond. Without embarking here and now upon a work of theology—which I am ill-prepared to undertake—I can only say that I doubt whether the existing churches are fitted to carry that message triumphantly through the world. It seems to me that there are certain figures that should find their places in the church, even if one follows the priesthood of all believers. There is the worker-priest. There is the mature man who wishes to take up the cure of souls after a worldly career. There is the monk, the nun, the friar; the travelling preacher; the social volunteer. How they might all fit together in a structure of missions or parishes I am not sure: perhaps they should not. But if God is what I think Him to be, then somewhere, before long, someone will launch the new Reformation that we need.

How, in my closing lines, to sum up the future of violence against which all this might be our defence? At times the outlook is terrifying. Life which, in the western world, seemed not so long ago to be one of steadily increasing comfort, now seems more and more perilous and uncertain. The ship no longer answers the helm. The rowers no longer obey their orders. The complications of urban life of which we were once so proud seem to have left us powerless against dissidents, saboteurs and assassins. Despised and neglected minorities are revived by the breath of international anarchism, and find new champions among the dynamic and under-employed student generation. Extreme cruelty is inflicted upon the innocent. Madness is mimicked as a revolutionary technique, and justified by grotesque perversions of reason. Total war now has a younger brother, total terror. The old traditions of law and order seem powerless to arrest it. Weapons of destruction move with increasing ease from the official armies to the semi-official underground. Which will be the first guerrilla group to threaten nuclear warfare? To shoot down a civilian airliner? Bomb a city from the air? Hold an entire school to ransom? Torture its victims live on television?

The terrorists already owe a debt to the bereaved that can never be paid: for the Munich Massacre, the Lydda Massacre, the twenty-nine in that Pan American jet incinerated at Rome Airport. And yet I still believe that this is really less an age of violence than most that have gone before it. Certainly there is more concern, a more passionate reaction against violence, than there has ever been. I believe that the level of violence is distorted by two factors: the mass media which (not without service to our cause) make every other shot heard round the world; and current weapons technology which has made violence so much more efficient. It took only four phosphorus grenades at Rome.

To any reader who wishes to think more about the problem of human aggression, I recommend the writings of Konrad Lorenz and Anthony Storr in particular. Yet no book written, this present one included, can ever have the last word on the subject. We still know far too little about violence as about so many other aspects of our glorious misery. If we spent half as much talent and money upon the working of our minds as we do upon the working of our bodies, we might live as happily as we now live long.

Book List

1. Gordon W. Allport in *Tensions That Cause War* ed. Hedley Cantril, University of Illinois Press, 1950.
2. Robert Ardrey *African Genesis*, Athenaeum, N.Y., 1961.
3. Robert Ardrey *The Territorial Imperative*, Collins, 1967.
4. Robert Ardrey *The Social Contract*, Collins, 1970.
5. Raymond Aron *On War*, Secker & Warburg, 1958.
6. Raymond Aron *War and Industrial Society*, Oxford University Press, 1958.
7. Roland Bainton *The Penguin History of Christianity*, Penguin, 1967.
8. Richard J. Barnet *Roots of War*, Athenaeum, N.Y., 1972.
9. *Bhagavad Gita*, various translations, especially Juan Mascaro, Penguin, 1962.
10. Eds. Leon Bramson & George W. Goethals *War*, Basic Books, London and New York, 1968.
11. J. Bronowski *The Face of Violence: an essay with a play*, Turnstile Press, 1954.
12. Alan Bullock *Hitler: A Study in Tyranny*, Harper, Revd. Edn., 1960.
13. Jacob Burckhardt *The Civilisation of the Renaissance in Italy*, Tr. Middlemore, Phaidon, 1944.
14. Carl von Clausewitz *On War*, Tr. Graham, Kegan Paul, 1918.
15. R. A. Derrick *A History of Fiji*, Govt. Press, Suva 1968
16. E. F. M. Durbin and John Bowlby *War and Democracy*, Kegan Paul, 1938.
17. Eisenhower Commission: James F. Kirkham, Sheldon G. Levy, William J. Crotty—*Staff Report to the National Commission on the Causes and Prevention of Violence*, Bantam, 1970.
18. Amitai Etzioni *Toward a Sociological Theory of Peace* in *Sociological Theories* ed. Llewellyn Gross, Harper & Row, N.Y., 1967.
19. *Mensch und Tier: Ausdrucksformen des Lebendigen* ed. Heinz Friedrich, Munich, 1968. Available as *Man & Animal*, tr. Nawiasky, Paladin, 1972.
20. Rene Fülop-Miller *The Mind and Face of Bolshevism*, Putnam, 1927.
21. *Selected Writings of Mahatma Gandhi*, ed. Ronald Duncan, Fontana, 1971.
22. Martha Gelhorn *The Face of War*, Sphere Books, 1967.
23. H. D. Graham and E. R. Gurr Violence in America: *Historical and Comparative Perspectives*, *A Report to the National Commission on the Causes and Prevention of Violence*, Bantam, N.Y., 1969.

24. Alan Harrington *Psychopaths*, Simon & Schuster, N.Y., 1972
25. Richard Hooker *Of the Laws of Ecclesiastical Polity*, Everyman's Library (Dent), 1925.
26. Edward Hyams *Killing No Murder*, Nelson & Sons, 1969.
27. *The Quaker Approach to Contemporary Problems*, ed. John Kavanaugh, Allen & Unwin, 1953.
28. Leonard C. Lewin *Report from Iron Mountain*, Macdonald, and Penguin Books, 1968.
29. Liddell Hart *Thoughts on War*, Faber & Faber, 1944. Also *Deterrent or Defence*, Stevens & Sons, 1960.
30. Konrad Lorenz *On Aggression*, tr. M. Latzke, Methuen, London, 1966.
31. William McDougall *An Introduction to Social Psychology*, Methuen, London, 1915.
32. Alasdair MacIntyre *Marcuse*, Fontana, 1970.
33. Niccolo Machiavelli *The Prince*, Oxford University Press, 1942.
34. Bronislav Malinowski *An Anthropological Analysis of War*, American Journal of Sociology XLVI, University of Chicago, 1941.
35. Mark A. May A Social *Psychology of War and Peace*, Yale University Press, 1943.
36. *The Pacifist Conscience*, anthology ed. Peter Mayer, Rupert Hart-Davis, London, 1966.
37. William Robert Miller *Nonviolence: A Christian Interpretation*, George Allen & Unwin, 1964.
38. Montgomery of Alamein *A History of Warfare*, Collins, 1968.
39. Desmond Morris *The Human Zoo*, Jonathan Cape, 1969.
40. Lewis Mumford *The Condition of Man*, Secker & Warburg, 1944
41. John U. Nef *War and Human Progress*, Routledge & Kegan Paul, 1950.
42–43. Friedrich Nietzsche *Twilight of the Idols* and *The Anti-Christ*, one volume, tr. R. J. Hollingdale, Penguin, 1968.
44. Thomas Paine *The Age of Reason*, Thinker's Library (Watts & Co.), 1938.
45. Winwood Reade *The Martyrdom of Man*, Thinker's Library (Watts & Co.), 1938.
46. John Searle *The Campus War*, Penguin, 1972.
47. J. H. Skolnik *The Politics of Protest, A report to the Eisenhower Commission on Violence*, Ballantine, N.Y., 1969.
48. George Sorel *Reflections on Violence*, tr. T. E. Hulme, Collier, N.Y., 1970.
49. Anthony Storr *Human Aggression*, Penguin 1968 (Pelican 1970).
50. Surgeon General's Scientific Advisory Committee on Television and Social Behaviour: *Television and Growing Up—The Impact of Televised Violence*, U.S. Department of Health, Education and Welfare, Washington, 1971.
51. George Thayer *The War Business*, Weidenfeld & Nicolson, 1969.
52. Lionel Tiger and Robin Fox *The Imperial Animal*, Secker & Warburg, 1972.
53. Edward C. Tolman *Drives Towards War*, Appleton-Century-Crofts N.Y., 1942.

54. Arnold Toynbee *A Study of History*, Abridgement of volumes VII–X by D. C. Somervell, Oxford University Press, 1957.
55. Alfred Vagts *A History of Militarism*, Hollis & Carter, 1959.
56. Geoffrey Vickers *Freedom in a Rocking Boat*, Pelican, 1972.
57. Colin Wilson *A Casebook of Murder*, Frewin, 1969.
58. Colin Wilson *Order of Assassins*, Rupert Hart-Davis, 1972.
59. Prof. Quincey Wright *A Study of War*, two volumes, University of Chicago Press, 1942.
60. Steven Runciman *A History of the Crusades*, three volumes, Cambridge 1951, Penguin Books (Pelican) 1971.
61. Eldridge Cleaver *Soul on Ice*, Dell: Delta Books, N.Y., 1968.
62. George H. Gorman *Introducing Quakers*, Friends Home Service Committee, London, 1970.
63. Religious Society of Friends *Advices and Queries*, pamphlet, Friends House, London, 1964.
64. David Caute *Fanon*, Collins: Fontana Modern Masters, 1970.
65. Andrew Sinclair *Guevara*, Collins: Fontana Modern Masters, 1970.
66. Cyril Falls *The Art of War*, Oxford University Press, 1961.
67. Donald Swann *The Space between the Bars*, Simon & Schuster, N.Y., 1961.
68. C. L. Sulzberger *An Age of Mediocrity*, Macmillan, N.Y., 1973.
69. Nirad C. Chaudhuri *The Continent of Circe*, Jaico, Bombay, 1966.
70. Wernher Maser *Hitler*, Allen Lane, 1973.

Encyclopaedia Britannica, Chicago, 1967.